Building Conservation Contracts and Grant Aid

A practical guide

KEN DAVEY
Formerly Chief Quantity Surveyor
and Head of Contracts at English Heritage

E & FN SPON

An Imprint of Chapman & Hall

London · New York · Tokyo · Melbourne · Madras

**Published by E & FN Spon, an imprint of Chapman & Hall,
2–6 Boundary Row, London SE1 8HN**

Chapman & Hall, 2–6 Boundary Row, London SE1 8HN, UK

Van Nostrand Reinhold Inc., 115 5th Avenue, New York NY10003, USA

Chapman & Hall Japan, Thomson Publishing Japan, Hirakawacho Nemoto Building, 7F, 1-7-11 Hirakawa-cho, Chiyoda-ku, Tokyo 102, Japan

Chapman & Hall Australia, Thomas Nelson Australia, 102 Dodds Street, South Melbourne, Victoria 3205, Australia

Chapman & Hall India, R. Seshadri, 32 Second Main Road, CIT East, Madras 600 035, India

First edition 1992

© 1992 Ken Davey

Typeset in 10 on 12pt Palatino by Best-set Typesetter Ltd
Printed and bound in Great Britain by Hartnolls Ltd, Bodmin

ISBN 0 419 17140 1   0 442 31466 3 (USA)

A catalogue record for this book is available from the British Library

Library of Congress Cataloging-in-Publication Data
Davey, Kenneth Jackson.
    Building conservation contracts and grant aid : a practical guide / Ken Davey.
    p.   cm.
    Includes index.
    ISBN 0–442–31466–3
    1. Construction contracts—Great Britain.   2. Historic buildings—Great Britain—Conservation and restoration.   3. Historic sites—Great Britain—Conservation and restoration.   4. Grants-in-aid—Great Britain.   I. Title.
KD1641.D38   1991
343.73'07869—dc20   91-23020
[347.3037869]   CIP

Contents

Preface

Conservation of our historic buildings, ancient towns and old villages
is now receiving more attention than ever before. The need for funding the cost of such important work, however modest or extensive
the scale of the project, requires examination in the practical context
of how best to set about the work and also how to give the client or
building owner the most value for money. Grant aid may sometimes
be available for the more important archaeological, historic or 'at risk'
properties or estates but many owners have to fund the cost of the
necessary constructional activities from their own resources. It is vitally
important, therefore, to ensure that the financial and contractual arrangements recommended to, and used by, an owner or organization
are going to give not only the desired results in terms of the best and
most suitable repair, consolidation or alteration, but that the work is
performed efficiently and within a sound and appropriate contractual
framework.

Many building professionals are excellent at producing proposals
for building conservation based on general concepts, sometimes aided
by sketches or drawings. A fewer number readily enjoy translating
such ideas of what needs to be done into a sound and comprehensive
specification. However the real weakness in the chain of events is that
too few architects, building surveyors, general practice surveyors,
quantity surveyors, planners, structural and civil engineers and conservation officers have had the opportunity to practise on the whole
range of available contractual options. An awareness of this range of
options, including the possible activities of directly employed craftsmen and others, needs to be considered if a client or building owner
is to be given best advice.

When dealing with something as sensitive as an individual historic
building, a group of buildings contained in a conservation area, or
indeed a much larger estate, then it is perhaps understandable that
many practitioners will tend to keep with the familiar and adopt a
method of procurement which they have used in the past. Although

this may produce a satisfactory contract it does not follow that it is the best solution. The proper approach is for the building professional to stand back and ask himself/herself what is the intended end result and, most importantly, what is the range of contractual options which should be considered in order for the end result to be achieved in the most satisfactory and cost effective manner?

It is something of a truism that a soundly based contract will often do much to help achieve the desired result in terms of building conservation while, at the same time, providing the optimum value for money. A contract which can be properly priced by a contractor, which gives the best value for money to the client, and which protects the legitimate interests of both contractor and client, will often proceed smoothly with mutual satisfaction all round.

This book is aimed, therefore, at the building professionals, many of whom are extremely competent and knowledgeable about the history of architecture, the recognition of different building styles, and with experience of building construction in all its many forms but who seek guidance or possibly reassurance on the whole range of contractual arrangements which are available to them and their clients. Similarly it attempts to give an understanding of the basic philosophy and application of grant aid. It is hoped that the content will be of help to the more experienced practitioners, those qualified but perhaps without an extensive knowledge of building conservation, and to those students who have the wish to gain a greater awareness of how building contracts involving conservation work may be tackled and possibly grant aided.

The need for a treatise such as this has been very much in my mind as a result of practical experience and particularly when attempting to grapple with ideas put forward by those new to building conservation work. An awareness of this need was reinforced when the College of Estate Management asked me to contribute on this subject which leads to the award of the RICS Postgraduate Diploma in Building Conservation. This book is a development of material prepared for the College of Estate Management and it is hoped that the content will be of help to a wider readership who are committed to conservation and who need to provide contractual or grant aid advice to their clients or other building owners.

This book is intended to fulfil the function of describing all the principal methods of arranging and letting building and civil engineering contracts for conservation work of virtually any type. Included is an introduction to the basics of building conservation such as the distinction between ordinary building work and conservation practice, the professionals and others involved, the role of the archaeologist, conservator and historian, observations on some repair techniques, an explanation of the terms 'consolidation' and 'leave as found', references to opening-up operations, staged working, scaffolding, protected species which may be encountered, archaeological finds, specifications in general, and other matters which are intended to introduce the reader to some of the special features of building conservation.

Other topics covered include contractor selection, the use of directly employed labour, and other considerations of particular relevance to building conservation work.

Since grant aid is often closely linked with some types of building conservation and with the consolidation or repair of scheduled monuments, it was decided to devote a part of the text to this important aspect of conservation.

Also included are appendices which cover such matters as practical examples of how to incorporate archaeological finds and daywork provisions into contracts. The appendices also list, with a commentary, those principal Conditions of Contract which are applicable to virtually any type of building conservation project. There is also an appendix listing the principal grant aid organizations or giving reference to appropriate sources of contact for further information.

Finally there is a glossary of terms which it is hoped will be helpful to those less familiar with some of the terminology used both in more straightforward constructional activities as well as in building conservation.

An effort has been made to keep the book free of unnecessary padding and it is intended to be a concise, authoritative and practical guide. If it helps in leading to a wider understanding of all the factors involved in recommending or selecting the most effective type of contractual arrangement for a given scheme and in giving a greater insight into grant aid, then it will have achieved its aim.

Ken Davey
Reigate

ABOUT THE AUTHOR

Ken Davey is a Fellow of the Royal Institution of Chartered Surveyors and a member of the Institution's Building Conservation Committee. He is also a board member helping to oversee the RICS/College of Estate Management Postgraduate Diploma in Building Conservation and was formerly Chief Quantity Surveyor and Head of Contracts at English Heritage. Currently he is in private practice specializing in building conservation contracts and grant aid.

PART ONE

Introduction

Chapter One

Introduction

Although many aspects of the letting of contracts for conservation work are similar to other non-conservation constructional activities, there are essential differences which call for special attention. For example, significant problems are created by the fact that the very location where work is to take place is almost certainly sensitive in a historical, architectural or archaeological sense – this has a fundamental influence on the way in which work is to proceed and in the use of the most appropriate type of contract, contractor or directly employed labour. Those new to conservation will soon become aware of the philosophical debate which can be engendered by activities associated with historic buildings, archaeological remains or town schemes where a whole area or neighbourhood is the subject of conservation work.

It is essential that the design team involved with a conservation project is made up of all the appropriate professions if the original structure, fabric, area or equivalent is to receive the respect it deserves.

On a non-historic project, the design team will normally be comprised of a designer, quantity surveyor, civil or structural engineer and mechanical and electrical engineer. On occasion there will also be input from other professions such as landscape architects.

With conservation work there has to be a greater flexibility over the professional involvement. Those involved must have a sympathy and expertise in the type of work envisaged together with a proper appreciation of the historic or archaeological relevance of the building, ancient remains or historic area where the works are to take place. Thus the normal range of professions which would be associated with a non-historic project need to be supplemented for conservation work by those with an understanding of the historic nature of the original structure and possibly also its internal finishings. This additional expertise comes from trained archaeologists (frequently referred to as inspectors), historians and conservators.

It is a common misconception to regard archaeologists as being concerned solely with ancient or historic remains which may be buried in the ground. In fact, many archaeologists are the real specialists in identifying the historic nature of a building, determining how it was put together, and describing the type and source of materials which would have been used when the original structure was constructed. It is the archaeologist who should often be looked to as possessing the necessary degree of knowledge about old buildings and remains and who can advise, so that an old structure is not effectively vandalized by well intentioned but ill-conceived repairs.

If furnishings or the internal fittings of a building are at risk, or in possible need of replacement or repair, then a conservator working closely with an archaeologist or historian will probably need to become involved.

Conservators and historians usually enjoy close links with the larger museums, many of which are of world renown, and appropriate advice should always be sought when the need arises.

The design team should possess, either collectively or individually, an in-depth understanding of traditional craft techniques and an appreciation of the use of modern technology such as alkoxy silane formulations for the consolidation of friable stone walling, epoxy resin liquids and grouts applied by hyperdermic syringe or injection gun, and mortar stitching treatment using epoxy resin mortars in conjunction with non-ferrous or glass fibre dowels to help save spalling or cracked masonry. These and other techniques are very much a part of present day conservation work.

With the larger historic buildings, particularly heavy masonry structures such as will be encountered in castles and equivalent ancient monuments, and the more complex timber framed structures, it is advisable to employ the services of a suitably experienced structural engineer. The words 'suitably experienced' were deliberately chosen: many structural engineers may not have had the opportunity to work on truly historic buildings and the possibility of extensive replacement may be anathema to those with the responsibility for the care of our historic built inheritance. To a degree the desire to embark on extensive replacement can be understood in engineering but not historic terms. Thus an engineer's inherent caution may lead to the historic value of a building being put at risk through over design of replacement parts. This is included here as a cautionary tale because there are structural engineers with suitable experience of historic repair work. It is no exaggeration to state that many a project involving the potential expenditure of extremely large sums of money has been able to proceed by using an appropriate consultant with the experience and confidence to declare an old building structurally sound after only minimum repairs have been carried out.

Another area of conservation work where there has been a distinct change in the pattern of repair is that needed when timbers are found to be infected with dry rot. In the past the generally recommended solution was to carry out the replacement of timbers well beyond the actual area of decay itself. It is now realised that if the source of the ingress of water can be removed then the replacement or repair of timbers can be greatly reduced; this is of particular importance on historically sensitive buildings and again appropriate independent professional advice can lead to reduced overall expenditure.

A problem frequently encountered with conservation work is the difficulty of actually identifying what needs to be done by way of repair. At this point it is appropriate to mention that much repair work on historic buildings and ancient monuments is referred to as 'consolidation'. On occasion the term consolidation is something of a misnomer but nevertheless it is a term which is widely used and therefore needs to be understood. Archaeologists and historians, when appraising an existing structure which is in need of repair (consolidation) invariably state that, so far as is possible the original structure must be left as found. This basic philosophy of 'leave as found' is fundamental to true conservation. Conservation effectively means the same thing as preservation and every effort should be made to retain what is truly historic and not attempt to improve on history. Any attempt to 'improve' old remains is artificial and would destroy the historic value of the original.

The philosophy of 'leave as found' has its counter arguments. For example, to what extent can the philosophy be applied to large public buildings which are required to have a working use as opposed to being a museum piece? It is doubtful if a large room which is to be used for banqueting purposes would be considered satisfactory by its users if missing pieces of an otherwise historic plaster cornice were not to be replaced. The most likely solution to this problem would be to retain the plaster cornice *in situ* as far as practicable and to fill in any gaps with identically matching sections. This latter approach will have its opponents who, rather than attempt to restore a building in as sensitive a manner as possible, would prefer to leave the missing pieces of the cornice out altogether so as not to compromise the historic integrity of the building.

It is probably true to say that the 'leave as found' approach is easier to apply to smaller scale domestic or industrial type buildings and to the larger museum type buildings or structures represented by the many ancient monuments such as castles, disused abbeys, old fortifications, Roman remains and pre-historic sites. In the case of the larger museum type buildings and structures it is most likely that they will tend to fall into a category of their own. This is because the original purpose for which they were constructed has usually long since passed and it is therefore easier, in many respects, to give absolute priority to apply 'leave as found' principles in a truly historic context to such structures.

There is a variant to the leave as found approach which is adopted on suitable buildings. This is to leave the sound portion of a structure or particular feature completely unaltered, apart possibly from re-securing, and to fill in gaps with pieces of material which whilst serving the dual purpose of helping to prevent further deterioration (for example by the ingress of water) and giving a good overall visual effect can be seen, on closer examination, as not attempting to constitute a facsimile copy of the original. There are examples of this sort of honest and sensitive restoration throughout the UK and abroad. A good recent example of this type of restoration may be seen at the gatehouse to Stokesay Castle, Shropshire, where the building is of timber frame construction and with much of the original exposed timberwork having a moulded shape. In the restoration of this building it was decided not to attempt to match the original mouldings but to replace missing or decayed woodwork with timbers of the same general overall dimension but without any attempt to reproduce the mouldings. The result on this early 17th century gatehouse has been to carefully restore in such a manner that to future generations – particularly those with an eye for detail and historic integrity – the original building will not have been compromised.

Those dealing with new building projects have the benefit of access to drawings and specifications before the building is actually constructed. Similarly such drawings and other design information is generally available when recently erected buildings have need of repair. Those dealing with conservation projects rarely have the benefit of access to original drawings; in many cases buildings were created by master craftsmen without the use of drawings as we understand them today. Even if drawings or sketches had been prepared for the larger and more important buildings of their age it is most likely that they will have long since disappeared with the passage of time. Nevertheless, on certain buildings which are now of historic interest, it is possible that research into local and/or national archives will produce some recorded evidence which can be put to good use when considering a programme of repair.

A frequent problem when surveying an existing structure is to determine the extent of the essential repairs required. This is particularly so when trying to ascertain the extent of the faults which lie concealed within the structure or which are high off the ground or otherwise in a difficult or inaccessible position. It is self evident that if it is difficult to determine the extent of the likely faults then it is even more difficult to attempt to specify the necessary remedial work. This difficulty of access, particularly in the past, was too readily used as an excuse to elect for the easy option, in contractual terms, of proposing that a contract should be let on a prime cost basis. There are occasions when either the whole or a part of a repair scheme has to be let on a prime cost basis but the disadvantages are such that all other options should be explored first before advising clients that it is in their interests to proceed on such a basis.

Given a project where identification of the faults is problematical and access is difficult then particularly careful attention needs to be given to the best type of contractual arrangement. The various types of contract are described later but, if at all possible, an attempt should be made to persuade the client that it may be financially beneficial to consider letting the work in more than one stage. By phasing the actual operations on site it is possible to give greater attention to finding out the root causes of any problems; invariably this is time well spent which will eventually result in much tighter financial control over the scheme as a whole.

If a staged method of proceeding with works activities is agreed upon then typically the first stage would be to create a contract for the initial exploratory work and opening up operations, possibly together with a means of temporary protection over the whole of the working area. Such a means of proceeding enables access to various otherwise concealed parts of the structure and facilitates the preparation of a proper schedule of repair based on the actual findings. The second stage would hopefully result in a firm price tender, or one of the other means of contracting which is described later, where cost is related to the physical quantity of work to be performed, and which in totality relates to the defects discovered during the separate stage one opening up operations. Given an experienced design team the period of elapsed time between the completion of the first stage and the commencement of the second need only be short. On some projects sufficient information will have been obtained from the early investigatory work that tenders for the main scheme of repair may be invited well in advance of actual physical completion on site of all the first stage operations.

The provision of scaffolding for access, inspection and actual works activities forms a significant part of the cost of repairs to historic buildings. The cost of temporary work is likely to be particularly high when a temporary roof is to be provided so that work may continue in otherwise adverse weather conditions.

Scaffolding may be a key factor in determining how a job is to proceed. Frequently the type of scaffolding to be provided is influenced by the decision as to whether an investigatory inspection is to be conducted in advance of the commencement of the major repairs to an external facade.

Temporary access scaffolding may be erected and dismantled at fairly reasonable cost to enable a proper survey of the external surfaces and/or internal fabric. Once the survey is complete then the temporary access scaffold which is usually of a lightweight nature or a portable type may be removed.

Since scaffolding costs usually involve hire charges for rental it is incumbent on those responsible for the actual site survey to ensure that personnel are on site, and in sufficient numbers, so that the client is not involved in unnecessary and prolonged hire charges.

Another method of proceeding is to enter into a separate initial contract for the erection of a working scaffold. This type of scaffolding may then be utilized for both the initial site survey and for the subsequent building activities. A disadvantage with this method is that considerable hire charges for a robust scaffold are incurred very early in the life of a project. Thus an initial and substantial expense is incurred during a period of time when the repair solutions are being considered, formulated and drafted, and with such expense extending through the tender period and before major building works can actually take place on site. An alternative solution, particularly if the contract is of long duration, is to take quantity surveying advice as to whether it might be more economical for the client to consider outright purchase of the scaffolding. In any event the contract documentation must clearly define the right of use, maintenance responsibility, the possible need for re-erection in different locations on site, and the final removal when the use of the scaffolding may be dispensed with. All the factors referred to here will have considerable cost significance.

Another matter which should be considered is whether protected species of mammals or rare plants exist on site or within the close vicinity of the working area. If a colony of bats or indeed any protected or rare species of wildlife, vegetation or flowers are known to be present on site then this is something which should be referred to in the contract documentation if contractual claims are to be avoided. This is because their presence could cause delay or disruption to the otherwise regular progress of the works and on which a contractor would have reasonably based his tender.

Archaeological finds are a distinct possibility on many historic sites. It is prudent to include in tender documentation a means of pricing the possible financial consequences of disruption or delay if such archaeological finds are the cause of either a total or partial stoppage of the works.

Whichever type of contractual arrangement is envisaged there will be the need for a clear statement of what is to be performed and how. This statement usually takes the form of a specification. To help avoid missing important items of activity, workmanship or materials from a specification, it is good practice to base a project specification on a suitable standard specification. The PSA General Specification and the National Building Specification (NBS) are typical examples of standard specifications which are readily available and which form a useful starting point for specification writing.

A standard specification aims to cover most types of constructional activity by an extensive list of optional clauses. The optional clauses generally cover a very wide range of materials and workmanship and also give examples of items for inclusion in preliminaries. When using a standard specification the author of the project specification selects those clauses which are relevant only to the scheme in hand and supplements these standard clauses by particular or supplementary clauses which are needed for the project but which do not appear in the standard specification. Practitioners involved in conservation will find that there is the need to introduce particular clauses of their own for inclusion in the project specification; over a period of time, a series of suitable specification clauses will accumulate which are then available for use on a needs basis.

Those new to conservation will find that there are excellent reference sources which may be used as the basis of drafting specification clauses. The five volume 'Practical Building Conservation Series' which is the product of the staff of the Research, Technical and Advisory Service of English Heritage, has recently set a standard which it will be hard to emulate or better in the field of conservation. The five volumes cover stone masonry; brick, terracotta and earth; plasters, mortars and renders; metals; and wood, glass and resins. Volume Five in this series also includes a bibliography giving useful references relating to the practical aspects of the repair, maintenance and conservation of historic buildings.

There are also numerous organizations dedicated to various aspects of conservation and membership of one or more of these organizations will provide the means of meeting fellow professionals with similar interests; this can be very helpful when a particular conservation problem is encountered for the first time. The Society for the Protection of Ancient Buildings (SPAB), and others, issue publications and arrange visits and courses, all of which can form an extremely useful aid to specification writing and the widening of an awareness of conservation matters.

The foregoing is intended as a general introduction to some of the particular things which will need to be considered on a conservation project. Since many of these items have cost implications to a contractor it is essential that they are adequately dealt with in whichever form of contract is decided upon.

PART TWO

Means of Procurement

Chapter Two

Lump sum contracts incorporating firm Bills of Quantities

A lump sum contract is precisely what it states. In return for a lump sum payment from a client to a contractor the contractor undertakes, when tendering, to perform the work which is encompassed within the tender documentation. That is not to say that the scope of the work and hence the final price will not vary. Almost certainly there will be changes of mind by the client or by the designer, or other changes in circumstances which, under the terms of the Conditions of Contract, give a contractor an entitlement to the adjustment of his originally quoted lump sum figure. The vehicle for obtaining the most accurate assessment of the likely final cost of a project is by using a professionally prepared firm Bill of Quantities which enables all the tenderers to compete on a fair and equitable basis.

A firm Bill of Quantities is a totally comprehensive contract document which lists all the activities which have to be performed and all the obligations which the successful contractor will be called upon to meet. Much of the work which lends itself to measurement is included in a Bill of Quantities by way of description. The descriptions are also accompanied by the actual extent or quantity of the items of work involved and these quantities of measurement are expressed in m^3 (cubic metres), m^2 (square metres), m (metres), or enumerated items. The precise unit of measurement adopted is dependent on the physical shape of the work involved.

It is the function of the quantity surveyor to prepare Bills of Quantities in accordance with a strict set of rules. The most common set of rules which is likely to be adopted for conservation work, and which has been agreed between the Royal Institution of Chartered Surveyors and the Building Employers Confederation, is known as the Standard Method of Measurement of Building Works: Seventh Edition. This set of rules became operative on 1 July 1988.

In addition to items of measurement a Bill of Quantities will include pricing points for all the many items known as 'preliminaries' and which do not lend themselves to measurement. Typical preliminaries will include such things as requirements in respect of the contractor's general obligations, setting out, supervision, liability for and possibly insurances in respect of injury to persons and property, access to the working area by others employed direct by the client, obligations and restrictions imposed by the client, temporary plant and equipment, scaffolding, transport of work people to and from the site, water, lighting and power for the works, temporary roads and other means of access, all temporary storage, hutting and similar facilities required by the contractor, temporary telephones, safety, health and welfare facilities, drying out, temporary fences, screens and similar items, anti-pollution measures and many other items which may attract a charge on the contract.

Bills of Quantities will also usually incorporate all work which is to be performed by nominated sub-contractors, provision for daywork (preferably introducing an element of competition into the way in which the daywork is to be priced), possibly pricing points for the financial consequences of either partial or total cessation of the works as a result of archaeological finds and, with some clients, an allowance for contingencies.

When preparing Bills of Quantities the quantity surveyor will collaborate closely with the rest of the design team whose task it is to prepare drawings, specifications and, frequently on complex conservation schemes, a separate schedule of work to be performed. On occasion, and despite a proper survey, it will be necessary to include 'provisional quantities' for those aspects of the job which cannot be precisely determined in advance. When the work is actually carried out in respect of any matters included in the Bills of Quantities by way of provisional quantities, then the quantity surveyor measures and agrees with the contractor the precise extent of the work involved and sets the cost of such activities against the provisional quantities as contained in the contract bills.

Bills of Quantities also frequently include provisional sums for items of work which cannot be decided upon in advance or which may occur but with no degree of certainty. Here, at final account stage, the quantity surveyor will set the actual values of the work performed against the lump sum provisional allowance included in the Bills of Quantities.

When it is known that certain specialist activities or materials are required and the designer wishes to exercise direct control over the selection of appropriate firms then it is customary to include such activities or specialist materials by way of prime cost sums in the Bills of Quantities. The contractor is given the opportunity, by way of pricing points, to allow for his own profit and attendance against such items in the bills.

Bills of Quantities should preferably be used on conservation contracts with an estimated value in excess of about £150 000. On smaller but complex projects it may also be to the client's advantage to consider using such documents. If there is any doubt about whether financial benefits are likely to accrue to the client by either using or dispensing with Bills of Quantities then advice should be sought from a quantity surveyor who is experienced in conservation work. It is possible that on smaller projects the quantity surveyor may recommend another means of letting the contract which will still provide the client with a good degree of financial protection. It must not be assumed that quantity surveyors are mainly engaged in the preparation of Bills of Quantities; their expertise spans all aspects of contractual and financial advice on construction related projects.

Tenders using Bills of Quantities are usually called for on either a firm price basis or on a fluctuation basis. Tenders of a firm price nature may reasonably be called for when a contract has a duration not exceeding two years. In a firm price contract the tenderers have to allow for the risk of all price movements in the cost of labour, materials, plant and other items. In some types of firm price contract there is a provision for enabling the contractor to be reimbursed for increases in labour related taxes or similar levies such as National Insurance contributions. This is because such 'labour tax matters' are imposed by Central Government and cannot possibly be foreseen by any tenderer.

Those tenders incorporating fluctuation or variation of price conditions are suitable for projects which are likely to exceed two years in duration. The philosophy over allowing price increase in such long term contracts is that it is considered to be unfair to expect tenderers to forecast or anticipate the movement in labour and material costs, and other costs, over such an extended period of time. Even if tenderers are prepared to quote on a lump sum basis for a contract of very long duration it is most likely that they would have to build into their tender prices such large sums to cater for possible inflation that it would prove to be uneconomic for the client. Sensible tendering allows for the risks to be properly shared between client and contractor.

Fluctuation or variation of price contracts permit reimbursement to a contractor of his increased costs incurred during the progression of a contract. These increased costs are usually recovered on a formula basis as described in the contract. Alternatively increased costs may be reimbursed on the proven net difference in the cost of labour and of listed materials. This latter method of calculating fluctuation in costs is accurate but tedious, requiring a detailed analysis of all time and wages sheets for workmen and of all invoices for the basic materials to which the fluctuation provisions apply.

In practice most clients wish or demand to know their likely financial commitment on a project before actually entering into a contract. Without doubt a contract based on Bills of Quantities, particularly when firm bills are provided, gives the client the greatest possible financial protection, an excellent indicator of the likely sum which will be due to a contractor (as at the date of tender) and is the preferred option for all pre-planned conservation projects. Nevertheless the client should be made aware, through his or her professional advisors, that he or she will be called upon to pay the difference in price for all variations and changes in the original scheme. Occasionally a scheme may be reduced in scope once a contract has been let and, in these circumstances, the quantity surveyor will ensure that the client only pays for that which properly falls due under the contract.

Most contracts which incorporate Bills of Quantities contain detailed provisions as to the means of paying for varied work. The normal basis of payment is at bill rates if the variation does not significantly alter the scope of the work involved and if the work which remains is performed in similar circumstances to that which was originally contemplated. If the varied work is similar but not identical to that described in the bills then work is normally paid for at rates *pro rata* to those in the Bills of Quantities. If the varied work includes items which cannot be properly related to bill items then such varied work is usually paid for on a measurement basis but at fair agreed rates. Such fair agreed rates are frequently referred to as 'star' rates. Finally, if the work is completely incapable of measurement then additional work may be paid for as daywork. Daywork involves payment on the basis of the actual costs involved plus appropriate tendered percentage additions to include overheads and profit and which should be stipulated in the tender documents. Contractors will usually be found to express a preference for payment on a daywork basis but there are risks to the client associated with this method of payment unless there is constant and effective monitoring and supervision by a clerk of works. The quantity surveyor will ensure that daywork is only permitted when work is physically incapable of measurement. Hence dayworks should be regarded as the exception rather than the norm.

The essential key documents in a lump sum contract incorporating Bills of Quantities are as follows.

1. Drawings.
2. Bills of Quantities.
3. Specification. It is good practice to make the specification a contract document since a full and proper description of workmanship and materials is really inseparable from the design process. Nevertheless not all the standard conditions of contract name the specification as a contract document.
4. Schedule of works (if available). This is a list of activities which lends itself to tabulation in schedule format. Such a schedule is frequently included in conservation work as an annex to the specification – alternatively it may be included as a separate document in its own right.
5. Conditions of contract. Usually standard conditions are used which stipulate the essential contractual responsibilities and liabilities of the parties to the contract.
6. Tender form.

Note. The above list may have to be supplemented by other documents depending on client requirements and the selected conditions of contract which are to be used.

Chapter Three

Contracts based on approximate Bills of Quantities

It is not uncommon for the pre-planning of a conservation project by way of the preparation of full and sufficient drawings and a sufficiently detailed specification to fall short of the standards required to enable a firm Bill of Quantities to be prepared. In these circumstances it is still possible to proceed obtaining the principal advantages of a firm bill but lacking some of the precision which is inherent in such a document. A contract incorporating approximate Bills of Quantities probably provides a client with the second best means of achieving financial control over a complex or large conservation contract.

The essential key documents which were previously described as being necessary for a lump sum contract incorporating firm Bills of Quantities are equally applicable to a contract incorporating approximate bills.

There are essentially two types of situation when approximate Bills of Quantities may be considered for contract purposes. Both situations call for slightly different nomenclature in the bill description. These are as follows.

1. When the general nature and scope of the work is known but the precise extent and quantity of the work cannot be determined prior to commencement of work on site. The pricing document involved here is known as a Bill of Approximate Quantities.
2. When the need to perform work is manifest but until extensive opening up has been performed on site it is difficult to define both the nature of the work and the quantity or extent of the work to be executed. The pricing document here is known as a Provisional Bill of Quantities.

From the foregoing distinction it will be apparent that, if possible, a contract let on the basis of a Bill of Approximate Quantities (where usually the quantities are likely to be the biggest variable) is to be preferred to a Provisional Bill of Quantities where both the nature of the work and the quantities involved are less certain.

The principal advantages of using approximate Bills of Quantities are that the contractors tendering have a proper and equitable pricing basis for submitting their tender offers, the client enjoys not only the benefit of soundly based competition but the contract incorporates a proper basis for dealing with interim valuations/certificates, and there is a proper contractual mechanism for arriving at the final cost of the works, which is related to the actual extent of the work performed.

With both types of approximate Bills of Quantities previously described there is the need for full quantity surveying involvement and the complete re-measurement of the work actually performed.

When recommending to a client the use of approximate Bills of Quantities it is necessary to make it clear that the bills can only be as good as the design information or other data on which they are based. The client should also be made aware that he will have to meet professional fees for both pre- and post-contract services.

The principal advantages of using an approximate bill may be briefly summarized as follows:

1. all contractors base their tenders on exactly the same information;
2. there is usually soundly based competition;
3. the pricing document is a flexible instrument which may generally be used to deal with changes in circumstances on site;
4. the contractor is paid on a measurement basis only for work actually performed, which is capable of being physically checked on site, and on the basis of pre-determined rates;
5. the pricing document aids the better assessment of interim valuations for payments on account;
6. work may frequently commence on site at an earlier date than with other means of contracting;
7. an approximate Bill of Quantities may include prime cost sums for nominated sub-contractors, provisional sums for work which is possibly foreseen but of a problematical nature, provisional sums for possible incidences of an unexpected but possible type, and for daywork when work is physically incapable of measurement and as a last resort it is necessary to pay for activities on a cost-plus basis.

The principal disadvantage which, as previously stated, should be declared to the client, is that the final sum due to the contractor will depend on the actual extent of the work which it is found necessary to perform. However, this disadvantage is not nearly so great as with a prime cost contract which is described later.

As with any conservation project, the client should be advised as to a suitable sum or percentage of the contract figure which it would be prudent to set aside for possible contingencies. No client will ever thank his professional advisors if they fail to advise him on this point. Funding and budgetary provision for a works project can only be properly provided for on the basis of sound professional advice. Indeed, failure to point out inherent risks in a conservation project might give grounds for claims of negligence.

By its very nature, some types of conservation work involve opening up a building before the full extent of the problems, and hence the cure, may be decided upon. Contracts based on approximate Bills of Quantities have a long track record and are a frequent way of proceeding. Other contractual options are described elsewhere.

Chapter Four

Lump sum contracts without Bills of Quantities

Bills of Quantities should only be dispensed with on the smaller and less complex conservation projects. As a generalization it will be found that Bills of Quantities are often dispensed with when the estimated value of a scheme falls below about £150 000. Even below this value there is often considerable advantage in preparing bills because of the keener competition they engender and the greater financial control they provide to the client. If there is any doubt as to the suitability or otherwise of Bills of Quantities on a smaller value project, particularly when expenditure is still likely to exceed £100 000, then advice should be obtained from a quantity surveyor as to the most suitable contractual arrangements.

The key documents for use on a lump sum contract without Bills of Quantities are:

1. drawings;
2. specification;
3. schedule of work (to supplement the specification);
4. schedule of rates (see below);
5. conditions of contract;
6. tender form.

It should be noted that the above list may need to be augmented by other documents depending on the conditions of contract to be used and on particular client requirements.

In the absence of Bills of Quantities the specification becomes a much more important document. The specification must be fully comprehensive in all respects. This need for a fully comprehensive document applies to the description of all materials to be used, standards of workmanship, and preliminaries.

If the contract drawings omit to show what is required and the specification insufficiently describes the materials, workmanship and preliminaries, then almost certainly the client will be faced with a claim for extra monies from the contractor.

The difficulty of not having a pricing basis for possible variations may be overcome, to some extent, by the contract incorporating a separate schedule of rates. Such a schedule may be prepared and issued as a tender document for pricing by all the firms invited to tender. Alternatively the tenderers may be required to produce their own schedule of rates either with their tender or upon request if their tender is being considered for acceptance.

A schedule of rates prepared for use with a lump sum contract should attempt to list out all the major activities, in measurement format, so that in the event of variations being ordered post-contract there will hopefully be a pricing basis for calculating part if not all of the cost of a variation.

The disadvantage of many schedules of rates prepared for use with this type of contract is that the schedules may have been prepared by personnel inexperienced in measurement techniques and with insufficient knowledge of contractors' prices. There is, therefore, a very strong case for seeking the help of a quantity surveyor in preparing a suitable schedule before going out to tender. Similarly quantity surveying advice in the examination of priced schedules and the rest of the tender documentation, particularly qualifications put forward by contractors, is strongly recommended if the client's financial interests are to be best protected.

A possible and practical solution to overcoming the production of unsatisfactory schedules of rates is to write into the contract that, in the event of variations occurring, they are to be measured and paid for on the basis of a stipulated and recognized source of pricing information. However this still calls for expertise in deciding upon the most appropriate source of pricing data.

Some practitioners prepare a tender summary or tender analysis for completion by the tenderers. This can prove a useful document provided it is prepared with great care. Such a tender summary needs to list all of the elements of work to be performed and should always include a 'sweeping up' item for pricing by the tenderers. This sweeping up item should typically be based on a form of words such as that referred to in the tender summary below.

An example of a simple tender summary for consolidation of parts of an ancient monument could take the following pattern.

TENDER SUMMARY

Element of Work Involved	**Price** £/p
(1) All work to the external walls of the North elevation (Specification clauses . . . to . . . inclusive).	
(2) Replacement of cast lead covering to roof of tower (Specification clauses . . . to . . . inclusive).	
(3) Overhaul all lead hopper heads and downpipes (Specification clauses . . . to . . . inclusive).	
(4) Include the Provisional Sum of £2,000 for excavating, examining and repairing existing surface water drainage system (Specification clause . . .).	2,000
(5) Allow for complying with all aspects of the Specification Preliminaries (Clauses . . . to . . . inclusive).	
(6) Include the Provisional Sum of £____ (calculated on the basis of the sheet/s attached) in the event that the discovery of archaeological remains causes a partial or total stoppage of the Works. *NB* Appropriately worded clauses need to be drafted to meet this eventuality so that an element of competition is involved. Appendix A may be amended and incorporated in the tender documents so that the total may be transferred to this Summary.	
(7) Include the Provisional Sum of £____ (calculated on the basis of the sheets attached) for Dayworks. *NB* Appropriately worded Daywork provisions need to be drafted to meet this requirement so that an element of competition is involved for Daywork rates and allowances. Appendix B may be amended and incorporated in the tender documents so that the total may be transferred to this Summary.	
(8) Allow here, if not elsewhere provided, for any other matters as may be shown on the Drawings, described in the Specification, or as may be required by the Conditions of Contract. *NB* This is the 'sweeping up' clause referred to in the text above.	____

TOTAL AS IN TENDER £ ____

This type of lump sum contract, as previously stated, is suitable for the smaller value, less complex project. It is also a type of contract which enables a client to know his likely financial commitment before entering into a contract. It will be necessary to advise the client to make separate provision to meet the risk of unforeseen circumstances by setting aside a suitable contingency allowance.

Although lump sum contracts without bills of quantities can and do proceed without any quantity surveying involvement it is becoming increasingly common practice, particularly with the larger and more sophisticated clients, to seek quantity surveying advice in respect of the contractual arrangements, the tender evaluation particularly where tenders are qualified, and at post-contract stage in dealing with valuations for interim certificates and in negotiating and agreeing the final account.

Chapter Five

Prime cost contracts

Prime cost contracts are also referred to as 'cost plus' contracts. The reason for the alternative name is that it clearly describes the nature of the financial arrangements.

The essence of a prime cost contract is that a contractor is reimbursed for the actual costs of labour, materials and plant and, in addition, receives a further sum to cover overheads and to provide the required level of profit.

Prime cost contracts usually permit the overheads and profit element, frequently but somewhat misleadingly referred to as a 'fee', to be either tendered for by way of a percentage addition on the basic costs of labour, materials and plant; or alternatively, quoted by way of a lump sum addition on such basic costs.

A prime cost contract provides little or no financial control over the final amount which will be payable by a client to a contractor and for this reason should only be used as a last resort. With prime cost there is no tendered for lump sum at the commencement of the works and the client has to pay whatever the actual costs amount to plus the previously agreed lump sum or percentage addition to cover the contractor's overheads and profit.

A quantity surveyor should, if possible, be employed on a contract of this nature and his advice obtained as to whether the contractor's entitlement to overheads and profit should be on the basis of a percentage addition or lump sum as previously described.

The lump sum addition has attractions if the likely total prime cost of a project can be estimated with any degree of accuracy. However, the very nature of a project which, because of its uncertainties has led to the adoption of prime cost, usually means that both the design team and the contractors tendering will have difficulty in deciding upon what represents a fair and reasonable lump sum for overheads and profit. Inevitably a situation will arise when there is either an under or over recovery of the margin for overheads and profit. It will be seen that although the client will know in advance what he will have to pay for on-costs and profit, such a lump sum method is speculative and, in reality, frequently amounts to a form of gambling on the likely basic costs which will be incurred. If the lump sum method of payment for overheads and profit is rejected then this leaves the alternative which is to apply a previously tendered or agreed percentage addition to the actual costs incurred for labour, materials and plant.

With the percentage method of payment for overheads and profit there is no incentive for a contractor to keep his costs to the minimum. The more he spends the greater will be his return in terms of profit.

If it proves difficult to properly pre-plan a project and prepare the necessary drawings, specifications and schedules, then it is frequently suggested that a prime cost contract is the only means of proceeding to contract. However, before making this decision and recommending accordingly, the client should be advised of the financial risks involved, the lack of certainty over the final sum which will become due and, if possible, they should be advised to limit the prime cost element to a preliminary investigatory contract so that a separate contract may be let on a more satisfactory basis for the major part of the works.

It will be apparent that when work is being paid for on a cost reimbursement basis then strict supervisory control needs to be exercised in the checking of time and wages sheets for all categories of labour, in the scrutiny of all delivery tickets and invoices for materials, ensuring that surplus and unnecessary materials are not ordered, and in closely monitoring the movement and periods of hire for all mechanical and non-mechanical plant which has to be paid for. Some contracts embody a clause which permits the SO to call for daily or periodic returns in respect of all labour, materials and plant. Such a clause should be rigidly enforced as an aid in endeavouring to avoid unnecessary waste and expenditure.

Typical problems associated with prime cost contracts include the following.

- The need for and difficulty over the strict monitoring of labour actually employed on site. Labour resources can fluctuate considerably; excess labour and unproductive labour can create an unfair financial burden on the client. Off-site labour at workshops and depots and workmen employed in driving vehicles are particularly difficult to monitor.
- Neither the SO nor client have any control over productivity. Time wasting activities and excessive stoppage for meal and tea breaks and for unfavourable weather are difficult to control.
- The cost of rectifying defective work tends to be paid for by the

client. Without constant on-site supervision and appropriate re-cording such remedial work can fail to be credited to the client.

- The necessity to monitor closely all materials actually required against those shown on delivery tickets and invoices takes a great deal of effort. It is not unknown for supplies to be diverted else-where. Surplus materials left over at the end of the contract also have some monetary value but may be difficult to recover.
- Plant hire is an expensive business at the best of times. There is rarely any real incentive for a contractor to keep such plant on site for the absolute minimum time. More time on site means greater charges for the client. The SO should consider ordering the removal of plant from site if its continued presence seems unnecessary or uneconomic. Strict records should be maintained of all charge-able plant, and these records should list the type and quantity of plant deployed, when first delivered, and when actually removed from site.

In practice there is usually no difficulty in finding contractors will-ing and able to enter into prime cost contracts. Some firms will be found to be scrupulously fair in their method of operation. Others will be less concerned with the client's financial interests and will find it difficult to prepare and produce the necessary financial documenta-tion required. On balance the potential risks to a client are such that, as previously stated, prime cost contracts should be regarded as a means of last resort.

Chapter Six

Contracts based on schedules of rates

This type of contract has the advantage that payment is related to the work actually and physically performed and paid for on the basis of a previously agreed schedule of rates.

A contract of this type must include quantity surveying input in the measurement and pricing of the work executed at pre-determined rates in the agreement.

Unlike a lump sum contract there is no contract sum at tender stage but there is an agreement as to the schedule of rates which will apply.

As with prime cost the client cannot be informed at the outset as to what his final financial commitment will be. However, unlike prime cost, the client will know that he will be called upon to make payment against only that work which has actually been performed and which has a physical presence and is checked on site by the quantity surveyor. In other words the client will derive the satisfaction of knowing that payment is truly work related.

Very often a fair degree of accuracy is possible in forecasting, at pre-tender or pre-contract stage, the likely change within which the final cost will fall. This, however, is dependent on the drawings and specification being sufficiently advanced so that the quantity surveyor is able to prepare approximate quantities for the work involved and to price these out on the basis of the proposed schedule of rates with sufficient allowances for a tenderer's likely percentage adjustment on or off the schedule rates and with further allowances to cater for possible daywork and contingencies.

The schedule of rates may either be tailor made to suit all likely measured items of work which are to be involved in the contract or may include a comprehensive standard work of reference such as the PSA schedule of rates (obtainable from HMSO) and which may be augmented, on work which includes ancient monuments and historic buildings, by the specially prepared Addendum Schedule of Rates which is only obtainable direct from the Historic Buildings and Monuments Commission for England (English Heritage). Other standard works such as one of the several annually produced price books could, after the inclusion of suitably worded explanatory notes, definitions and rulings, also become the agreed schedule of rates.

If time permits it is preferable to have a comprehensive schedule of rates prepared for the particular project. This will have the advantage that only items relevant to the job need to be included in the schedule.

The design team, on the advice of the quantity surveyor, should decide at an early stage, whether a pre-priced schedule of rates is to form part of the tender package and incorporating a facility for tenderers to quote their own percentage adjustments on or off the pre-priced items.

The advantage of having a pre-priced schedule is that it simplifies matters at tender stage. The contractors tendering will only have to submit, as part of their offer, the percentage adjustment which they require on the pre-priced document. Nevertheless the tenderers will have needed to examine the pre-priced document and possibly obtained quotations from their own domestic sub-contractors before they are able to calculate the percentage adjustment which is required as part of the formal tender offer.

A different method of proceeding is to have quantity surveyor prepared schedules containing the full descriptions of the measured items but leaving all the items unpriced. Such a schedule is then issued to the tenderers who are then required to insert their own rates against each item. This alternative method provides tenderers with the opportunity to fine tune the rates to be inserted in the schedule so as to suit their own method of pricing and to reflect more accurately the rates they themselves will have obtained in competition from their own domestic sub-contractors. A disadvantage to this alternative method of pricing occurs at tender evaluation stage when the quantity surveyor will have to examine and analyse each tenderer's priced schedule of rates in order to determine which tender offers the client the most advantageous balance of rates. The tender evaluation can become very complex and to be truly fair and effective the quantity surveyor should have previously prepared, prior to receipt of tenders, his own assessment of the quantities or weighting factors which must be applied to each individual item, or group of items, which appears in the unpriced schedule. It is not simply a question of calculating the totality of the individual items which are priced in the tenderer's schedules – such a method would fail to give appropriate weighting to those items which are to form a greater part of the cost of a project. In effect, by adopting a suitable means of 'weighting' the quantity surveyor is able to arrive at the equivalent of the 'best buy' based on the individual rates offered multiplied by the frequency (quantity) each such item is likely to be used.

The method whereby standard pre-printed and pre-priced schedules of rates are incorporated into contracts has much to commend it, particularly if time is short. Nevertheless the quantity surveyor should always be prepared to identify any special elements of work not listed in the standard schedule but which it is known are likely to occur on a particular conservation project. It is then necessary to prepare a supplementary priced schedule to specifically cover those items which do not appear in the standard schedule.

Schedules of rates also form the basis of measured term contracts and their use in such situations is dealt with separately in Chapter 7.

Chapter Seven

Measured term contracts

Appendix G gives a general indication of the basis of a measured term contract (MTC). It is, quite simply, a contract where payment is related to the measurement of work actually performed and where the contract period spans a pre-determined period of time. An MTC is essentially a particular type of schedule of rates contract.

The use of an MTC is usually limited to a carefully defined geographic spread of different sites or to a single large estate where works activities are required. It follows that such contracts tend to be limited to the large property holding organizations such as the Property Services Agency (PSA) and English Heritage where there is frequently a constant demand for works activities of one sort or another on the estates for which they are responsible. In the case of the two organizations mentioned, the historic buildings and ancient monuments which are in their care amount to well over 2000 different locations. An MTC is equally applicable to any large property holding company where the buildings are reasonably close together and there is a continual demand for repairs, new works or both.

An MTC, properly used, provides great flexibility for the SO responsible for placing orders for work on a contractor. The SO is able to raise individual and separate orders or instructions for work either to fit a programme of planned maintenance or to meet sudden one-off requirements such as emergency repairs. However, all the orders placed on a contractor should comply with the customary minimum and maximum order value which is referred to below.

The SO raising an order for work on a contractor has a responsibility to ensure that each order contains or is accompanied by all necessary information needed by the contractor to perform the work. Typically there will be references to the building, the location where the work is to be performed and drawings, sketches and sufficient specification notes so that each order effectively becomes a mini contract within the principal MTC.

Daywork may be ordered within an MTC but its use should be strictly limited to those situations where the work is not physically measurable.

Specialist work to be performed by nominated sub-contractors may usually also be ordered on an MTC, the contractor being reimbursed for any necessary attendance on the nominated sub-contractor either by measurement and pricing at appropriate rates and/or on a daywork basis if measurement is impracticable. In addition the MTC Conditions of Contract should make provision for the contractor to be paid a percentage addition to cover overheads and profit on the proper invoice cost of such nominations.

JUSTIFICATION OF AN MTC

Before a group of sites or a single large estate justifies the setting up of an MTC there are a number of criteria which need to be satisfied.

1. The proposed contract must be of sufficient value; usually an annual expenditure in excess of £75 000 is needed before an MTC is justified. Preferably the estimated annual expenditure (EAV) should be greater than this sum so as to make the contract sufficiently attractive to contractors.
2. The client will have to provide staff or appoint consultants capable of specifying the work, raising orders, supervising the contractor, dealing with applications for payments on account and performing the measurement and pricing function leading up to the settlement of the final account for each separate order.
3. There must be a continuity of work to make this type of contract worthwhile so as to generate a contractor's interest. Continuity or a continued presence of experienced workmen on site is also generally in the client's interests. On some types of work there may be a learning curve on the part of the contractor's workforce so continuity is something which may benefit the client.
4. If it is the intention to group a number of different sites or estates into a single MTC then they should all be located within reasonable travelling distance of each other and of the contractor's premises or depot. This is because work may be switched from one site or estate to another depending on the requirements which arise. In practical terms a maximum travelling distance of one hour from a centrally located position should be aimed for or, expressed slightly differently, try to ensure that the most distant location of works activities does not exceed about 30 miles from

a convenient town from which suitable contractors operate. If travelling time or the distance to be travelled exceeds these norms, then it is to be expected that it will have an adverse effect on the tender prices. In the event that excessive travelling seems likely then the solution is either to set up a separate MTC for the adjoining area or to cater for isolated and more distant sites by separate lump sum contracts or other suitable but separate contractual arrangements.

5. The work must be capable of being properly managed and supervised on the client's behalf. The SO must have sufficient expertise to be able to specify the work to be performed, the facility to be able to raise individual orders and the ability to properly and directly supervise the site operations or to exercise this function through a resident or visiting clerk of works.

6. It should be recognized that each individual order must be self-sufficient since, in effect, each order constitutes a mini contract in its own right subject only to the terms and conditions of the principal measured term contract.

7. It will be essential to appoint a quantity surveyor to act on the client's behalf. His duties will be to interpret the schedule of rates and other contract conditions, jointly measure with the contractor the actual work performed against each order and, whenever possible, to price the work on the basis of the schedule of rates. The agreement of interim payments on account is usually left to the discretion of the SO but on the larger or more complex orders the quantity surveyor may be asked to perform this function on the SO's behalf.

8. The client must be prepared to enter into a contractual arrangement which spans a sufficient period of time (the term). In practice a three year term is standard for most MTCs, but see below.

9. When tendering for what is largely an unknown package of work and with a contract period likely to span three years, it is customary to introduce a break clause into the contract. Such a break clause is included in all Governmental MTCs. A typical break clause would permit a contractor to terminate the contract after having given three to six months notice of such intention. Similarly, if the client (usually on the advice of the SO) is dissatisfied with the contractor's performance then the contract can be terminated after having given the contractor the same amount of notice.

10. Because work may be scattered between different sites it would be unfair on the contractor to raise orders for trivial items since the transport costs alone could well exceed his contractual financial

entitlement when measured and valued on the basis of the schedule of rates. Similarly, larger one-off packages of work which, in normal circumstances, might be expected to attract keener prices should also be excluded from an MTC. The device contained in an MTC to overcome the problem of particularly small or particularly large value orders is to stipulate in the contract what is known as 'minimum order values' and 'maximum order values'. Work which falls outside this value range is excluded from the MTC. Such exclusion does not prevent a client (or SO acting on behalf of the client) to issue instructions to the same contractor and to pay for very minor items below the minimum order value on a jobbing or other agreed basis. Likewise those larger jobs may also be placed with the sitting contractor but as a separate contract and on terms to be agreed. Minimum and maximum order values can have a critical influence on the way in which contractors tender for MTCs, and the advice of a quantity surveyor should always be obtained.

UPDATING OF RATES

Because MTCs are entered into for a customary term of three years it will be necessary to make provision within the contract for updating the prices contained in the schedule of rates. Obviously the payment for an order which would have been acceptable to a contractor for work performed at or near the commencement of an MTC will become increasingly less attractive, or indeed loss making, unless provision is written into the contract whereby increases in the cost of labour, materials and plant can be passed on to the contractor. The means by which this is achieved is known as 'indexing'. This is to say that a price level index at the date of tender is established and movements in the index, either up or down, result in appropriate adjustments to the prices contained in the schedule of rates.

It is customary in MTCs to build into the contract appropriate provision for the monthly or other periodic updating of rates. This updating reflects any movements in the index. The PSA prepares, and the BRE publishes, a regular series of monthly updates for indexes for specific use with their own MTCs. This monthly updating is obtainable by subscription from the BRE, Watford, Hertfordshire.

It is worth noting that the English Heritage 'Addendum Schedule of Rates', which has previously been referred to, shares the same base date as the PSA schedule of rates. This serves the extremely useful purpose that both documents may be included as the basis of a contract since the monthly updated figures published by the BRE will be equally applicable to both schedules.

In addition to the normal updating, the various tenderers quote, in competition, the percentage adjustment which they require on the pre-priced schedules of rates. The successful contractor's entitlement to payment is therefore a combination of the following:

- work performed based on measurement and priced out at the rates in the contract schedule of rates; plus
- updating, expressed as a percentage; plus
- the tendered percentage adjustment.

The actual date of each order raised under an MTC determines the level of updating which is applicable to that particular order. Thus, with a governmental type contract, if the base index for the schedule of rates is 100% (when expressed as a percentage) and the BRE up-dating tables for the same schedule shows plus 18.4% for the month when the order was raised, this means that the rates extracted from the schedule of rates must be increased by 18.4% before applying the contractor's own tendered for percentage adjustment. If a contractor fails to carry out the work expeditiously they will normally only have a contractual entitlement to payment related to the index value or per-centage adjustment applicable at the date of the order and not that applicable to a subsequent month.

It should be noted that by far the greatest users of MTCs are organ-izations such as the PSA and English Heritage and the text substan-tially reflects this widespread usage. For many years they have used the Governmental Form C1501 General Conditions of Contract for Measured Term Contracts although, in the case of English Heritage, they have modified the conditions to suit their own particular re-quirements. In 1989 the JCT introduced their own Standard Form of Measured Term Contract which is referred to in Appendix C. With the JCT MTC Conditions the user is at liberty to elect for orders to be paid for either on a fluctuations basis which needs to be described, or, alternatively, on a fixed price basis which is really only suitable for MTCs of short duration.

Chapter Eight

Daywork term contracts

This type of contractual arrangement is used when, after considering the possible use of alternative forms of contracting, including an MTC, it is found that work cannot be pre-planned and that it is unlikely to be capable of payment on a measurement basis. Having ruled out an MTC and other options, then recourse may have to be made to a day-work term contract as a possible but much less accountable method of proceeding.

As with an MTC, a daywork term contract is for a period of time (the term) which is often three years. However the term may be varied to suit the particular circumstances, and the contract should include a break clause so that either party may bring the contract to an end as with an MTC.

Payment to a contractor is on the basis of daywork which should have previously been the subject of competitive tendering or negotiation.

Daywork is the means of reimbursing a contractor his actual costs for labour, materials and plant. In addition the contractor is customarily required to quote a percentage addition which he requires for overheads and profit. Some proposals require tenderers to quote hourly 'all in' rates for the differing categories of labour likely to be employed instead of a percentage addition on basic labour rates.

In a typical tender offer for daywork there might well be separate and different hourly rates for craftsmen and labourers. Means of paying for apprentices, young male labourers and any YTS personnel should all be covered by the tender documentation. Means of updating the hourly rates will also have to be considered, and this particular matter is avoided if the alternative method of a percentage addition on basic labour costs is the cost reimbursement procedure adopted.

Material costs are usually paid for on the basis of invoices provided but the contract should stipulate who receives the benefits of trade and cash discounts on such purchases. It is customary to ensure that the client receives the benefit of all discounts except perhaps a cash discount of $2\frac{1}{2}\%$ or 5% to encourage prompt payment to suppliers. In the instance of a contractor providing materials from his own stock then the contract conditions should stipulate the basis of payment; frequently this is at market prices prevailing at the date of delivery to the site. Handling charges may also be involved with the use of ex-stock materials; this point must be closely watched.

PLANT

Plant, both mechanical and non-mechanical, may prove somewhat burdensome to deal with. The contract should stipulate those items of non-mechanical plant such as small hand tools which are to be covered by way of the contractor's percentage addition for overheads and profit. Similarly the agreement must be equally clear about those items which may be charged for separately. It is common practice for the larger and more expensive items of non-mechanical plant such as scaffolding and hutting to be eligible for payment. In any event, the terms of the daywork agreement must be explicit so that disputes are avoided.

The use of mechanical plant invariably creates a situation giving the contractor an entitlement to payment. However many agreements will draw a distinction between the rates of payment for mechanical plant which the contractor obtains from a plant hire company and those items of mechanical plant which he provides from his own resources.

The two documents which are most commonly used and which provide a basis of payment for plant in Daywork are:

- *The Definition of Prime Cost of Daywork Carried Out Under a Building Contract* (a joint RICS and BEC publication);
- *Schedule of Basic Plant Charges for Use in Connection with Daywork Under a Building Contract* (an RICS publication).

Other documents which may be encountered and which provide definitions and rates for daywork include the *Definition of Prime Cost of Building Works of a Jobbing or Maintenance Character* (joint RICS and BEC) and the *Schedules of Dayworks Carried Out Incidental to Contract Work* (as prepared by the Federation of Civil Engineering Contractors).

Reference to the document entitled *The Definition of Prime Cost of Daywork Carried Out Under a Building Contract* will show that it was produced for use on daywork which is incidental to other work forming part of a larger lump sum contract. Nevertheless it is common practice for the document to be written into daywork term contracts.

From the above it is seen that a daywork term contract is similar in most respects to the category of work previously referred to under the title of 'prime cost contracts'. Nevertheless the essential and fundamental difference is that, as implied by its title, a daywork term contract is for a specific period of time (the term) and where continuity of work may be expected, perhaps over more than one site.

A daywork term contract suffers from the same lack of strict financial control as previously referred to for prime cost contracts. However, if each order raised on a daywork term contract is closely monitored and the contractor invoices for each order with the minimum of delay, then some degree of financial monitoring is possible. Also if the work is principally labour intensive and the size of workforce fairly constant, then a pattern of expenditure should begin to emerge which can be used, and projected, to compare likely expenditure with budgeted allocations.

Chapter Nine

Jobbing orders

Jobbing is merely a means of placing instructions for minor works to be performed by a contractor with the minimum of paperwork. It is possible to issue instructions for simple one-off jobbing orders (i.e. small and discrete packages of work) or a series of separate orders all placed on the same contractor. However, the benefits of competition and economies of scale are likely to be lost if a series of jobbing orders is issued instead of letting a larger and more comprehensive contract on the basis of properly prepared documentation.

In conservation there will be instances of small value but important items of work when time is of the essence and there is no real justification for preparing detailed contract documentation. Provided the client and/or his professional advisors are able to properly describe the work to be performed then offers on the basis of an exchange of letters or even verbal offers may be perfectly feasible and would be legally binding. Nevertheless it is essential to limit contracts of this nature to relatively minor activities where the risk is small if changes occur in the scope of the work. If things go wrong then verbal agreements in particular may become difficult to enforce or untangle and they are frequently the cause of disagreement or misunderstanding between the parties.

Jobbing may be ordered on the basis of agreed lump sums, on a daywork basis, or on some other basis provided the agreement makes it perfectly clear exactly what is to be performed and precisely how the contractor will be paid.

One aspect of particular difficulty with jobbing is the responsibility for making good defects in the work performed by the contractor. Another difficulty is if the contractor causes damage to the existing building or its contents as a result of his activities. These and other responsibilities are well defined in a project which incorporates one of the standard conditions of contract. With jobbing it is rare for either party to be protected by a binding agreement that clearly spells out the liabilities and responsibilities of the two contracting parties, and it is therefore necessary to fully understand the risks as well as the benefits if called upon to advise on such minor works.

Because of some of the pitfalls described above it is customary for larger clients, particularly those with the benefit of professional advisors, to impose a limit on the value of work which may be performed by way of jobbing orders. A typical financial limit would be to restrict jobbing to work which has an estimated value of under £500. However, if the supervisory staff acting on the client's behalf are adequately experienced, both in their ability to order and supervise jobbing work and also in a capacity to exercise financial control, then a client may be content to adopt a more relaxed attitude over the permitted maximum value of work which may be dealt with by way of jobbing. Obviously the independent client will be able to set his own rules and financial limits but, if asked, the professional advisor must always point out the potential disadvantages and risks involved as well as the advantages of minimizing the amount of paperwork and enabling an earlier presence of the contractor on site.

Chapter Ten

Management fee contracts

The initiative for Management Fee Contracts (MFCs) has arisen from a gap perceived by contractors in the construction procurement process. This response has partly arisen as a result of the actual problems which clients have experienced when faced with the apparent proliferation of different professional interests, the occasionally apparent uncoordinated activities between the design disciplines and main contractors, and frequently their awareness of the problems inherent in the nomination of specialist sub-contractors and suppliers – particularly under the complex procedures of the JCT Standard Form of Building Contract 1980 edition, and the general lack of co-ordination and strong leadership. It could be argued, and to an extent it is true, that contractors who are engaged in MFCs have merely filled a vacuum left by the uncoordinated efforts of the professions themselves. Many clients do not want to be involved in the selection of a large team of different professionals whose activities and functions are not particularly clear to them.

Even when clients are contemplating the use of a management contractor they are still at liberty and would be well advised to employ their own quantity surveyor and design consultant. Although the roles of these professional advisors will not follow the normal pattern associated with traditional contracting methods, the quantity surveyor will be able to advise on any suggested conditions of contract, the overall financial arrangements and will pay particular attention to clauses which could be activated in the event of the inevitable variations occurring. Similarly a client's independent design consultant will be available to advise on design criteria, design solutions and performance requirements.

SELECTING A CONTRACTOR

To a client the concept of employing a contractor with practical experience and management of the building process to oversee and take responsibility for the works activities frequently appears attractive. The term 'buildability' is used in the context of a contractor's proven experience of creating a complete building from start to finish. A comparison between creating a new building and undertaking and completing a conservation project may be held to be equally valid in terms of 'buildability'. There is no doubt that experienced contractors employed in a management role on behalf of the client bring a wealth and depth of experience of the procurement process to the benefit of the client. However, it must be understood that a contractor's principal responsibility is to his shareholders, or the equivalent, and it does not follow that the client benefits to the same degree as when he engages his own independent professional advisors whose allegience is solely to him.

A management fee contractor should be selected on the basis of a proven track record in the type of scheme being contemplated and also must be able to demonstrate that their organization possesses, in depth, all the different levels of managerial and technical skills which are needed for the proposed task. The contractor should also be required to show that other contracts have been successfully completed, on time, and to budget costs.

In return for a previously tendered or negotiated fee a management contractor will be responsible for all works activities which are to take place and he will be responsible for the letting, supervision and overall control of all elements of the job on the client's behalf.

It is good practice, and is now becoming customary, to interview prospective management contractors so as to ascertain their track record and suitability for handling and completing the project to the previously mentioned criteria of quality, time and cost. At the interview emphasis is likely to be placed on the managerial capacity of the firm and whether or not they are able to offer any particular skills or expertise. The interview panel should comprise the client, or his representative, the client's quantity surveyor and any design consultants the client proposes to employ. It should be kept in mind that the larger contractors are able to deploy personnel at these meetings who have been particularly selected for their ability to make highly professional presentations on behalf of their employers. It is therefore necessary to have a check-list of those questions which are of the greatest interest to the client and to receive satisfactory assurances in respect of the extent and experience of the on-site supervision and visiting managerial staff which would be allocated to the contract. On conservation work it is essential that those in charge of the project have a proper grasp of basic conservation philosophy and of the conservation techniques which are likely to be needed.

To be of interest to the larger contractors, however, the size of project has to be of sufficient value to generate their interest. Few management contractors will be interested in projects with an estimated value of below £1 million and most firms would be looking towards a much higher contract value to justify their involvement.

JOB DESCRIPTION/DEMARCATION

The management fee contractor's task will be to organize and obtain competitive tenders for the site set-up costs. These will include the normal range of essential preliminaries such as temporary roads, hutting, security, fencing, lighting, water, public health and site supervisory roles (the latter may or may not be covered elsewhere in the management fee). Additionally the management contractor will be required to suggest names of suitable specialist contractors for each element, section or trade involved. These lists of names may be supplemented by others put forward by the client or his independent consultants but the management contractor should be allowed a wide measure of discretion over the names of likely specialist contractors since it will be his responsibility to ensure compliance with his programme and standards of performance. There are 'horses for courses' and the management contractor will be in frequent contact with a wide range of sub-contractors and will know those best placed to undertake work of a particular type and at a particular time.

Once tender lists are agreed for suitable specialist contractors then competitive tenders are invited either on the basis of bills of quantities or on another suitable basis. The client will then enter into a contract or series of contracts with all the specialist firms involved and their work will come under the direct monitoring, supervision and control of the management contractor.

The client is responsible for paying the actual final cost of each subcontractor's work as negotiated and agreed by the management contractor or as negotiated and agreed by the client's quantity surveyor (if such a consultant is employed). The management contractor may be entitled to charge, depending on the terms of his agreement, a previously agreed lump sum or percentage addition on each separate specialist contract. There are, or should be, no hidden discounts, and it is in the interests of the contractor's reputation that projects are satisfactorily completed, on target, and within the predetermined budget.

The involvement of large national contractors in conservation related management fee contracting is probably much greater than is generally realised. An example of large scale management fee contracting took place in Liverpool when, for a variety of political and environmental reasons, it was decided to refurbish, in a truly authentic manner, a whole series of Georgian terraces in an effort to regenerate what had become a very run-down and neglected area. In this instance there was a considerable injection of public money from central government by way of very generous grant aid to a large number of individual property owners. This left the individual owners merely having to provide a small percentage of the total cost. The vehicle for this particular project was a management fee contract where the contractor was required to deploy a whole range of skills in contacting all the interested parties and obtaining their co-operation and involvement, in addition to providing the equivalent of professional services in such matters as design, specification, tendering arrangements, the letting of a wide variety of separate contracts for different trades, site supervision, through to the settlement of final accounts for each property, and the necessary close liaison with the agents acting on behalf of central government. This example is perhaps untypical insofar as the high level of grant aid which was made available. Nevertheless it serves to illustrate how town schemes of a conservation nature may be tackled by local authorities or others with the assistance of grant aid and using a management fee contract as the basis of proceeding.

ADVANTAGES AND BALANCE OF RISK

One of the principal advantages of a management fee contract is that it can be arranged so that there is no other pecuniary interest to the management contractor outside his agreed management fee. The question of payment of a lump sum or percentage addition on the cost of specialist works is very much a matter for negotiation between client and management contractor. Having established at the outset what payment is to be paid to the management contractor, he is free to direct his efforts to controlling the job in the best interests of the client and without having to devote the customary attention to his own profit margins as with normal contracting.

A management contractor will have a permanent presence on site and should be well placed to deal with any emergencies or difficulties which may arise. The contractor's staff will be particularly good at dealing with tradesmen in a manner and language which they readily understand.

Most of the contractors engaged in management fee contracting are larger firms who operate on a regional or nationwide basis and who have the capability and resources to engage in this type of work. Some of the firms involved have set up separate subsidiary companies to specifically deal with management contracting.

The balance of risk in management fee contracting is that the client has to accept most of the financial risks of contracting. This is unlike normal lump sum contracts where the contractor accepts most of the financial risks under the terms of such a contract. Because of this shift in the balance of risk it will be found that the fee required by management contractors is frequently in low single figures. The precise level at which the fee bid is pitched will depend very much on the likely duration of the contract and its estimated value. These last two factors determine the amount of staff and management involvement which a management contractor will have to deploy and hence greatly influence the fee required.

As a generalization a contractor will aim for a higher return on traditional lump sum contracting as compared with management fee contracting. This is because, as already stated, the contractor is taking most of the financial risks in lump sum contracting and expects commensurately higher rewards to compensate for such risks. With management fee contracting, as with prime cost, the contractor is at little or no risk unless he performs negligently.

On occasion a client will look to a management fee contractor to provide design resources or the equivalent of other professional services in which case the management fee will be considerably higher. Some clients may well look to a management contractor to provide a very wide range of ancillary services even to the extent of helping towards putting together a package of works which may involve a larger number of different properties with the added difficulty of perhaps being in separate ownership.

Chapter Eleven

Other forms of contract

There remain other forms of contractual arrangement including package deals of various sorts, 'turnkey' contracts, and schemes based on design, develop and construct methodology. In general these other types of contractual arrangement are not particularly well suited to sensitive conservation work on historic buildings and ancient monuments. For this reason they are not referred to here in greater detail. High speed fast track methods and industrialized technology are generally totally inappropriate to conservation work. True conservation will usually embrace the best facets of the 'leave as found' philosophy using traditional craft skills carefully employed to match the original fabric both in technology and, when possible, in the materials used.

PART THREE

Financial Control

Chapter Twelve

Financial control in respect of conservation contracts

The extent of financial control which is possible with the various types of contractual arrangement previously described is illustrated in the following diagram. It commences, at the top end of the diagram, with those contracts which, in general, give the least measure of financial control and ends, with those at the bottom, where the client derives maximum financial protection.

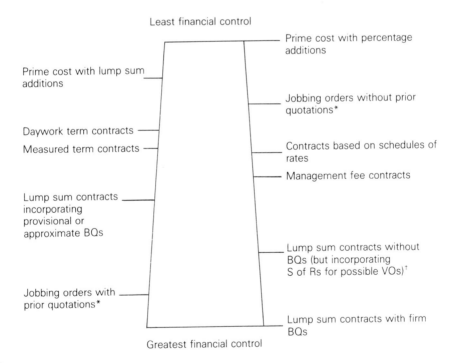

Least financial control

Prime cost with percentage additions

Prime cost with lump sum additions

Jobbing orders without prior quotations*

Daywork term contracts

Measured term contracts

Contracts based on schedules of rates

Management fee contracts

Lump sum contracts incorporating provisional or approximate BQs

Lump sum contracts without BQs (but incorporating S of Rs for possible VOs)†

Jobbing orders with prior quotations*

Lump sum contracts with firm BQs

Greatest financial control

*Contracts only suitable for minor works projects.
†Contracts suitable only for projects not exceeding approximately £150 000 in value.

To exercise financial control requires the use of appropriate professional expertise. It is recommended that, in the client's interests, a quantity surveyor should always be engaged in the following types of contractual arrangement:

- prime cost with percentage additions;
- prime cost with lump sum additions;
- daywork term contracts;
- measured term contracts;
- management fee contracts;
- lump sum contracts incorporating provisional or approximate bills of quantities;
- lump sum contracts with firm bills of quantities.

It follows that the remaining types of contract may be let without a quantity surveyor's involvement. Nevertheless many clients still ask for quantity surveying advice particularly when they seek reassurance on the contractual arrangements, professional help in monitoring and controlling financial commitments, and in the settlement of contractors' accounts. To be effective, financial control needs to be exercised at the following various stages of a project.

- Initial conception. Including discussions with client and clarification of brief.
- Feasibility stage. Production of possible outline design/repair solutions. Further discussions with client.
- Preliminary sketch plan stage. A development of the favoured scheme for the client's approval.
- Working drawing stage or equivalent. The preparation of detailed designs, working drawings, schedules of work to be performed, specification and possibly also the preparation of bills of quantities.
- Pre-tender estimate. A forecast of the likely lowest tender.
- Tender estimate stage. A reconciliation of the pre-tender estimate with the actual tenders received.
- Post-contract financial control. This can embrace a number of separate tasks such as:
  (a) valuations and certificates for interim payments to the contractor;
  (b) monthly or other periodic forecast of likely final cost – this will normally only occur on the larger schemes;
  (c) preparation and agreement of the final account with the contractor;
  (d) claims, if any.

The treatment of each of the above stages of financial control and of the various operations described are beyond the scope of this book.

Similarly cost planning techniques which are used by quantity surveyors, principally on new buildings or major refurbishment contracts, are also of too specialized a nature to be included here.

Although quantity surveying techniques are not dealt with, it is, however, essential that all professionals associated with conservation work are fully conversant with the general principles relating to client liaison, the roles of all other disciplines likely to be involved, the means of preparing sketches, drawings, schedules and specifications ready for incorporation into contract documentation, and the varied roles which a contractor may be called upon to perform. Furthermore the principal consultants need to be able to advise clients of the various ways of undertaking conservation work and possess the capability of being able to recommend the best and most appropriate contractual arrangements for the job in hand. Building professionals must be fully aware of how to invite tenders, prepare tender lists and receive and evaluate tenders. Additionally they must know how to perform or be capable of instructing others in the post-contract duties of preparing interim valuations and certificates for payments on account, periodic forecasts of costs so that clients are kept informed of their financial commitments, preparing and agreeing the final account with the contractor (which will include the adjustment of all authorized variations, the adjustment of prime cost and provisional sums, and the adjustment of any provisional quantities). The principal consultants will also be called upon to deal with applications from contractors for extensions of time in the contract period, advising on liquidated damages, offering advice or making decisions in respect of the interpretation to be placed on any of the contract documents including the relevant conditions of contract, and the means of resolving any claims which may arise and which are generally classified as contractual, extra-contractual or ex-gratia claims.

One particularly important matter associated with the financial control of building conservation contracts is the need to discuss and agree with the client a suitable allowance which should be set aside for contingencies. The question of contingencies is dealt with at greater length in Chapter 15.

Archaeological finds which may be regarded as part of the contingency sum and the separate daywork allowances which are also part of contingencies are similarly covered in Chapter 15. Appendices A and B give examples of how these two matters may be dealt with contractually.

PART FOUR

Contractor Selection

Chapter Thirteen

Contractor selection

The best planned and specified project will fail if insufficient attention is given to the contractors who are to be invited to tender. This cannot be emphasized too strongly because our built inheritance is at risk if contractors with insufficient conservation or management skills are employed. Against this must be carefully weighed the client's financial resources and ability to pay since it would be improper to only invite tenders from firms of national repute in the conservation field when perfectly competent contractors already operate in the area in which the site is located.

It must be kept in mind that once damage has been caused to a historic building or ancient monument then the original historic or archaeological value of the original structure may have become substantially or even totally lost as part of our heritage. This places great responsibility on those involved in the selection of contractors for this type of work.

It will be apparent that not all old buildings are of equal archaeological or historic interest. Their listing or scheduling status will vary and indeed some may be fairly old but of little archaeological, architectural or historic merit.

When considering potential tenderers every effort should be made to match the skills available from contractors with the quality of work to be performed. Whilst it is essential to use only the most highly skilled craftsmen on truly sensitive buildings, it would be patently absurd and a waste of money to employ firms only undertaking work to the highest standards on projects where such standards are not justified. The employment of over-qualified craftsmen is somewhat akin to using an unnecessarily high specification of requirements on a mundane building where such a specification amounts to extravagance. Put simply, the selection of potential tenderers should be on the basis of 'horses for courses'. It should also be remembered that some conservation skills are scarce and they should therefore be deployed where the need is greatest. In some instances contracts may have to be delayed until appropriate skills are available.

Before attempting to prepare a tender list it would be wise, if new to the area where the works are to be performed, to make enquiries of fellow professionals with local knowledge. Branches of professional societies such as the RIBA and RICS may be a useful contact. Others who may be approached for recommendations would include local archaeological societies, conservation officers employed by local authorities, and professionals employed by countrywide organizations such as English Heritage and the National Trust. An approach could also be made to the Conservation Group of the RICS. Investigation will reveal a body of interest and learning in most parts of the UK and similar organizations exist overseas since conservation is not limited to the UK but has worldwide ramifications.

Very often the best information may be gleaned from personal observation. A slow drive around the vicinity of the proposed works or the nearest town will often reveal the nameboards of firms who are possibly already performing work of a somewhat similar type and to an acceptable standard.

If there are any doubts about the capability of a firm then references should be called for and examples of their work examined. It will sometimes happen that a contractor, in all honesty and with a modicum of pride, will show an example of his work which although extremely sound and well constructed in terms of modern technology, displays a total lack of understanding and sympathy for historic workmanship and materials. Many craftsmen attempt to improve on history and this is often totally alien to sensitive restoration and consolidation 'work.

The size and expertise of contractors must also be matched to the size and complexity of the proposed project. Small local firms may be perfectly capable and ideal for dealing with the smaller scale domestic or industrial building and perhaps have a record of having repaired the local church. However, such a firm may be totally unsuited for employment on larger or more complex projects.

The balance of a contractor's permanent workforce, the extent to which he employs apprentices, and the degree to which he sub-lets specialist trades all need to be considered.

On the larger or more complex projects it is essential to consider the management skills which a contractor will be able to deploy. A suitable track record should be looked for.

Conservation can, and frequently does, involve both building and civil engineering activities and this balance of expertise should be available from potential tenderers when the job demands. Many jobs of a conservation nature will be found to be basically civil engineering in character. Typical examples of this sort would include the consolidation of ancient tunnels and watercourses (frequently associated with old abbeys), the repair of aqueducts and viaducts, work to heavy masonry structures including piling and other geotectonic devices, work to medieval sea defences, operations to support listed seaside piers, dredging of lakes and ponds on historic estates, and the stabilization of famous features such as the cliffs of Dover.

In carrying out conservation work the client will obviously be looking for value for money and this will only be achieved if economic factors are taken into consideration. The proximity of the site to the nearest town containing likely contractors is highly relevant. Whenever possible, local contractors are to be preferred for tendering purposes. In practice those firms which do not have to transport workmen for more than one hour to reach the site, or those which are within a radius of thirty miles of the site are to be preferred to contractors of equivalent calibre but which have considerable distances to travel. Travelling to and from the site is totally unproductive but is a cost which will be charged to the client irrespective of the form of contractual arrangement. Predilection towards particular firms or an unwillingness to investigate local or unknown contractors who may be perfectly suitable for the project must be guarded against.

From time to time a professional practice, local authority or other employing organization will be approached by general or main contractors and also specialist firms with a view to their name being included in future tender lists. The larger employing organizations, because they are awarding contracts on a frequent basis, will need to maintain some form of approved list or lists of contractors. In any event, whether the contractors make the initial enquiry or whether the client organization or practice adopts an approved list, it is necessary to compile data about all those who wish to be considered for future work.

When compiling records of firms it is necessary to adopt a structured approach to the questions which need to be asked. Additionally it is also a requirement to ensure that all information provided by a firm is regarded as confidential. This latter requirement is important because the answers to questions could possibly have a commercial use to their competitors.

The appendices include two questionnaires which could be used as the basis for issue to contractors and specialists. Appendix D is a questionnaire which is appropriate for issue to general contractors involved in conservation work. Appendix E is a shortened version of Appendix D and is more suitable for issue to specialists whose sphere of operation is limited to a particular craft operation. When completed and returned it will be found that the questionnaires provide the employing organizations with a lot of background information which is relevant when considering the suitability of a firm. Nevertheless it must be emphasized that a completed questionnaire is no substitute for personal examination of work already performed. This examination will involve site visits and should be conducted by a suitable professional, or by a small team of professionals, who should visit the sites of previous activities. References, if quoted, should also be taken up since not all circumstances are apparent from a visual inspection.

The design team will have established the scope and nature of the work to be performed before proceeding to seek tenders. In addition to identifying potential tenderers, the design team has a responsibility to ensure that competitive tenders are obtained from firms of broadly equivalent type suitable for the size and value of the project. It is both unfair and eventually a waste of time and money to pit large national contractors against small local firms. There is usually an optimum size of project for all contractors where they are likely to operate at maximum efficiency. It is also important never to include a firm in a tender list if, by so doing, they are merely included to make the number of tenderers reach a particular figure. All firms tendering should be doing so on an equal basis and on the understanding that all are quoting on an equivalent footing. If a firm is good enough to be invited to tender then the firm should be good enough to be awarded the contract if theirs is the lowest tender received. It is unethical to invite tenders and then proceed in accepting other than the lowest unless there are particular circumstances for so doing. In publicly funded projects such procedure would not be countenanced.

The number of firms invited to tender should be sufficient to ensure that the client, having properly tested the market, obtains competitive tenders which provide value for money. On small schemes there should be a minimum of three contractors tendering but, as the value or complexity increases, so should the number of firms invited to tender increase. Four is possibly a satisfactory number of tenderers for a job in excess of £50 000 and up to about £100 000. For schemes beyond £100 000 the number should be increased to five. On multi-million pound schemes there is rarely the need to increase the tender list for conservation work to more than five firms, but the client's wishes should always be taken into account. Some organizations invite tenders without setting any limit on the number involved. This is unfair because of the high cost of tendering and because of the low success rate which is inevitable. Once this sort of practice becomes known amongst contractors then invitations to tender from such a source are more likely to be declined or dealt with in a less enthusiastic manner.

Having referred to the preferred number of contractors to be invited to tender it needs to be remembered that, because of market forces, it is not always easy to obtain a fully satisfactory list of firms prepared to submit genuine offers.

Occasionally some contractors submit 'cover prices', but this is an improper practice and involves contact between tenderers and the disclosure, adjustment or fixing of prices. It is sometimes difficult to know when tender offers are genuine or not and the instances of cases of price fixing or similar malpractices which appear in the courts should be sufficient warning that the tender process requires the utmost vigilance. To give peace of mind over the levels of tenders received some clients, particularly the larger and more sophisticated organizations, always call for a pre-tender estimate of the likely lowest tender to be provided by a quantity surveyor in advance of tenders being received: this is good practice. When a quantity surveyor is involved in other pre-contract services then the provision of such a forecast may readily be written into his commission.

When the tender documents are ready for issue it is advisable to telephone all those firms who have previously expressed an interest in tendering to check that they are still interested. This is necessary because many contractors will frequently be involved in submitting tenders for a variety of jobs and, if they have met with a run of success elsewhere, then it would be in no one's interest if they were to become over committed. Such over commitment could possibly lead to either a poorer service or an inflated price, or both. When a firm is contacted and asks to be excused from tendering then their openness is to be commended and should not be an impediment to them being given additional invitations to tender in the future.

When making preliminary enquiries of potential tenderers, as much factual information as possible should be made available to them. Apart from location the contractors will wish to know the approximate order of cost or be given information so that they may prepare their own assessment. They will also be interested in the general nature of the works, the anticipated 'start-on-site' date and the contract period.

A factor which will greatly interest any potential tenderer is the permitted contract period. Time also greatly influences cost. If the period set is too short then contractors may either decline to tender or may have to increase their prices to allow for uneconomic working and/or overtime payments to workmen. Likewise if the contract period is too long then the contractors may be involved with extended preliminaries and other on-costs. There is usually an optimum time for most contracts and clients should be persuaded that it is in their best financial interests to set realistic contract periods.

Once tender documents have been issued it is common practice to find that tenderers will seek clarification on matters which may affect their tenders. Care must be taken, when responding to such enquiries, that information given to one firm does not place them in a privileged position. If the matter raised is likely to be of interest to other tenderers then an appropriate notice should be issued to all tenderers.

When tenders are in, it is customary to closely examine the lowest tender received. Certainly in the case of contracts incorporating bills of quantities it should normally only be necessary to examine the priced bills submitted by the lowest tenderer. During the tender examination stage all tender anomalies should be discussed and resolved with the lowest tenderer. Any matters which need to be confirmed should be confirmed in writing. The quantity surveyor or other professional advisor is then in a position to make a formal recommendation of acceptance to the client. Formal acceptance by the client should then follow as quickly as possible.

PART FIVE

Directly Employed Labour

Chapter Fourteen

The use of directly employed labour

Directly employed labour (DEL) tends only to be used by major property holding companies, the larger local authorities and cathedral works organizations. In the conservation field, however, several hundred craftsmen are employed throughout England by English Heritage.

There are distinct advantages and disadvantages with DEL operations.

The advantages

- Labour is always available for sudden emergency repairs.
- Skills which are in particularly short supply may be developed by an enlightened use of apprentices and on the job training.
- Workmanship of a consistently high quality may be expected because of a constant involvement with conservation work under experienced professional and technical supervision.
- Supervision required is frequently less because the workmen involved will have gained wide experience in the use of traditional skills and in the application of conservation techniques.
- There is a caring approach to their work. Craftsmen readily identify with and tend to take a pride in their association with buildings or monuments which are part of our heritage.
- There is a ready source of recruitment for craftsmen of the right aptitude to take on the supervision and training of apprentices and others who are less skilled.
- May be used to help outside organizations on an occasional and appropriate cost reimbursement basis. On occasions DEL craftsmen from publicly funded organizations may be deployed in the private sector in lieu of grant aid.

The disadvantages

- There is an unavoidable source of expenditure to their employer. The employer of DEL has to pay for his workmen even if the weather conditions during winter months and other periods of bad weather make normal constructional activities impossible. This contrasts with the same employer's use of a contractor where payment is normally job related.
- Mobility of DEL operatives has been a problem with some organizations. There has been a tendency to recruit labour for a limited area of operations or even for a particular estate. When work patterns change this can lead to difficulties.
- Productivity may be less than that achieved by contractors' workmen whose output is frequently enhanced by bonus or incentive schemes.
- Less conscientious workmen may come to regard their jobs as an appointment for the remainder of their working lives; motivation is then difficult.
- Staff retention can lead to difficulties. This is because DEL tend to be employed in the public sector where total remuneration is often lower than in the private sector. If an organization operates an inflexible wages structure this can lead to unbalanced gangs of workmen. Clearly an unbalanced workforce cannot operate efficiently and is thus closely related to the productivity of the group as a whole.

On large estates the situation frequently arises that permanent DEL resources are inadequate to cope with an unexpected increase in workload. In this situation it is necessary to supplement the DEL resources by bringing in suitable contractors. However, contractors should be awarded discrete packages of work so as to avoid the potential for demarcation and similar disputes.

The large estates will almost certainly involve a fluctuating workload irrespective of whether or not a system of planned maintenance is operated. Here, given the presence on site of DEL, the most economic solution might be to use the DEL resources for a clearly defined package of work which has an element of continuity and to bring in contractors for the occasional special project. This arrangement, which is well proven, provides a flexibility which is particularly effective in both managerial and financial terms. It also avoids having to maintain an excess of DEL staff who might otherwise be less than gainfully employed.

To be effective the management of DEL requires a permanent core of supervisors at various levels. The supervision and management must be in capable and experienced hands which have the capability of overseeing the work, ordering materials and carrying out the more simple surveying tasks.

The decision to operate a DEL organization involves a commitment to paying for the associated costs of maintaining suitable offices, mess-rooms, workshops, storage facilities and a plant depot, together with a responsibility for the payment of rates and electricity for power and lighting. The facilities which must be provided for a DEL operation are essentially the same as those which a contractor would have to provide in order to run a comparable commercial business.

One aspect of the management of DEL resources which requires particular attention concerns the provision of information to the work-force. To be efficient a DEL workforce must be provided with drawings, sketches, specification notes and other relevant information about the work to be performed. This information should be of an equivalent quality to that which would be required and provided to a contractor. The fact that DEL are an 'in house' resource should not permit sloppy standards, and there is no real excuse for providing such a workforce with less than the necessary level of supervision and management.

If called upon to advise in respect of DEL operations it is essential to start off with the premise that the effectiveness and morale of a DEL organization is most likely to be effected by its top management. Such management should always be in the hands of those possessing a thorough knowledge of the construction industry. A workforce will feel more secure and contented, and therefore more likely to be efficient, if it knows that it has a management which is appropriated qualified, understands the problems of the particular crafts, and has a proven record of management within the construction industry.

PART SIX

Particular Contractual Considerations

Chapter Fifteen

Contractual considerations of particular relevance to conservation work

INTRODUCTION

Before proceeding with this chapter, it is necessary to fully understand the matters contained in chapter one. Chapter one and this chapter, when taken together, will help in a better understanding of some of the basic principles which are described below.

Any construction project should be soundly based contractually, and a building professional of any discipline has the duty of care to ensure that his client receives sound, relevant and up-to-date advice. If for no other reason the client should be advised, in most instances, that a formal contract will need to be arranged and that this will impose obligations on both the contractor and himself. If the client is unaccustomed to being involved in works contracts then it would be time well spent taking him through the various key clauses contained in the recommended conditions of contract. In this way there should be no problems in respect of such matters as payments to the contractor, insurances, the principal liabilities of the two parties, and the relationship of the principal participants, i.e. client, contractor, SO, quantity surveyor, clerk of works/resident engineer and possibly others such as archaeologists, inspectors, historians and conservators who may be involved in work on a historic building or ancient monument but who are not specifically referred to in the standard contract conditions. It is necessary for the client to understand that the contractor is responsible for the performance of his or her own work, for the work of his or her domestic sub-contractors, for the co-ordination of specialist trades and sub-contractors, and for ordering and installing any specialist materials which may be included in the contract. The client should be made aware that the general administration of the contract on his behalf will be looked after by the SO (whose powers are usually listed in the conditions of contract) and who may or may not be assisted by a clerk of works and/or resident engineer. Only the SO should be responsible for giving instructions to the contractor although it is customary to delegate some powers to the clerk of works/resident engineer particularly with regard to the replacement of anything which does not comply with the drawings or specification or which is defective. The client should be advised that if he wishes to introduce any changes then he should always work through the SO and not give instructions direct to the contractor. On the larger or more complex projects there will be a quantity surveyor who, acting on the client's behalf, deals with all financial matters arising including the preparation of valuations for interim payments, preparing periodic forecasts of cost (if part of the commission), and the measurement, pricing, negotiation and agreement of the final account with the contractor.

Many if not all of the contractor's obligations are listed in the preliminaries section of the bills of quantities or alternatively will be described in the specification. These documents should cross refer to the relevant conditions of contract which are to apply. The preliminaries section of a typical bill of quantities will contain pricing points for tenderers to insert their rates and allowances against all the many conditions of contract and the various preliminaries involved.

PRELIMINARIES

Preliminaries, where in bills of quantities or specifications, or in both, are very important. Matters which should be considered or covered in preliminaries for a conservation project are as follows.

Project title
This should be as meaningful as possible.

Parties
At tender stage this will be limited to the name of the client.

Names of consultants
These should be listed and will often appear on the front covers of the bills of quantities and specifications.

Description of the site
Clear directions of how to locate and reach the site should be given. A site location plan accompanying the tender documents is always very helpful.

Access to the site
On a conservation site or in a conservation area it is essential that all contractor's traffic is strictly limited to pre-determined routes. In some instances there will be the need for prior consultation with archaeologists or others to ensure that ancient remains or sites of special scientific interest, including rare plants or animal life, are not damaged or disturbed. The probability of encountering rare species of plants or protected animal life is always greater on a conservation site, particularly when in a remote or little-visited locality.

Working area for the works
This, together with any allocated space for temporary storage facilities, hutting of all kinds and plant must be very carefully defined if possible damage to a historic fabric or to ancient remains is to be avoided. On a conservation site it is always advisable to show on drawings the areas to which a contractor will be confined. On occasion irreparable damage has been caused by contractors' workmen being allowed to stray from loosely defined designated areas and inadvertently causing damage to a highly sensitive part of a historic fabric or interior.

Adjacent buildings
These should be referred to and any particular constraints which are to apply must be listed. Frequently adjacent buildings which are not the subject of the works may be of equal or greater historic or archaeological value than those on the site.

Mining or other subsidence
On occasion an old building or structure may have suffered damage prior to the contractor entering the site. A full condition survey should be prepared and preferably issued as part of the tender documents. This avoids possible disagreement at a later date as to whether or not the contractor is responsible for certain defects.

The works
There must be a good description of the scope of the works to be performed. Any particular historic or archaeological features which are

present in an existing structure should be brought to the contractor's attention. Working in and around buildings or remains which are listed or scheduled always requires greater care and hence results in higher costs. It is customary to include drawings indicating the general scope of the works when tender documents are issued.

Sequence of execution of the works

This may be of importance for a number of reasons which are particular to the job in hand. Clients' stipulations must always be referred to. Typical instances occur when buildings are already in occupation and it is necessary to arrange the work with the minimum of inconvenience to the owners, occupants and visitors. Most constructional activities involve a measure of inconvenience to others but all possible efforts should be taken to keep such inconvenience to a minimum.

On the larger conservation contracts it is common practice to arrange the works in stages. Each such stage must be carefully defined in the documentation. It is important to ensure that work performed in later stages carefully matches that performed in earlier stages and that all stages bear a proper relationship to the existing structure and its finishings and exterior.

Phased work frequently requires the contract documentation to stipulate separate start and completion dates (or periods of time) for each stage, the need for each phase to be priced separately in the tender, and the requirement for separate amounts of liquidated damages to be calculated and entered in the tender documents.

It is most important to note that if the contract documentation is silent on the question of phasing the works then it will be reasonably and properly assumed by contractors that they may perform the works in an order best suited to their own methods of operation. If at a later stage the client or SO attempts to introduce a phased or staged method of proceeding to meet the client's requirements then almost certainly the contractor will have a valid claim for extra costs because of the possible prolongation or disruption arising as a direct result of the change in the original basis of the contract.

Conditions of contract

These are dealt with in greater detail below.

CONDITIONS OF CONTRACT

Typically a project will include, as part of the contract, a comprehensive set of standard conditions. It is recommended that quantity sur-

veying advice is taken at an early stage as to the most appropriate conditions to be used. Although standard conditions of contract are comprehensive when used for the type of project for which they were created there are, inevitably, certain instances or particular clients who wish to incorporate extra requirements of their own or who may wish to modify, delete or add to existing standard conditions. To avoid the whole of the standard conditions of contract having to be re-printed to meet such a need, it is common practice to introduce any such modifications, deletions or insertions to standard conditions by way of 'supplementary conditions of contract'. Such supplementary conditions must be referred to in the tender invitation listing the contract documents and also in the letter of acceptance. Because of their non-standard nature supplementary conditions should be issued to all contractors tendering.

The conditions of contract which apply must be stated in the tender documents. Where bills of quantities are used it is normal practice to list out in the preliminaries section of the bills a complete list of all conditions together with their abbreviated titles or headings. This is so as to provide a convenient pricing point for the tenderers to include a sum of money for each such obligation or condition. The fact that a tenderer has not inserted a sum of money against each such item should not be taken as implying that it has no value – the method of pricing a bill of quantities is entirely at the discretion of a tenderer and he may choose not to reveal his pricing techniques in certain respects.

A typical set of contract conditions will include references and pricing points for all of the following or their equivalents.

Definitions of terms
A list to be used within the conditions.

Contractor satisfaction
Contractors must satisfy themselves as to the site and all matters affecting the execution of the works.

Unforeseeable ground conditions
This may appear in some sets of conditions and gives a contractor the right to extra payment if the ground conditions actually encountered are such that they could not have been reasonably contemplated when tendering.

Vesting of works etc. in the client
Such a condition gives the client a title to both the partially and wholly completed works. It is also common practice to include within such a

condition a proviso to the effect that things are not to be removed from the site by the contractor without prior consent having been obtained. This proviso is particularly valuable if there is any possibility of a contractor becoming insolvent and it also guards against a contractor removing unfixed materials from a site when they may have already been paid for in a certificate.

Specifications, drawings and bills of quantities

The contractual validity of these is generally covered by the conditions. For those less familiar with works activities it is pertinent to know that the specification is, or should be, a detailed description of the materials to be used and the standard or quality of workmanship required. Drawings should be sufficient to show the extent and nature of the works so that when the specification and drawings are read together a contractor has all the information necessary for him to perform the works required. A bill of quantities is a professionally prepared pricing document which gives, in a required format, a totally comprehensive description of the works in an analytical manner which enables tenderers to price each and every part of the project on the same basis.

The relevant contract conditions must be consulted to see whether the specification, drawings and bills of quantities are all deemed to be contract documents or not. With some conditions of contract the specification is not named as a contract document although how such an integral part of the design process can be excluded is difficult to rationalize. On smaller or less complex projects a bill of quantities is unlikely to be called for.

It is worth noting that when a specification or bill of quantities includes something which is contrary to something stated in the conditions of contract, then the conditions normally take precedence over the other documents.

Schedules of repairs and schedules prepared for similar purposes may not be specifically referred to in the contract conditions. Such schedules may easily become contract documents if they are given a series of drawing numbers and included with the other contract drawings. Another convenient approach with schedules is to have them bound into either the specification or the bills of quantities.

It should be noted that in the private sector it has become common practice for some firms not to prepare properly detailed specifications and to leave the quantity surveyor to cover this loophole by giving descriptions of materials and workmanship by way of preambles in the bills of quantities. An examination of the terms and conditions relating to the consultancy appointment for the design element may indicate that this practice is questionable. On work for governmental departments and agencies it is recognized that the specification is an essential

and integral part of the design process and accordingly a specification is insisted upon and has to be provided by the architect, building surveyor, engineer or other responsible professional as appropriate. With the introduction of the industry-wide sponsored Co-ordinated Project Information (CPI) it is likely that the private sector will be increasingly urged to follow the procedures used by governmental departments, English Heritage and similar public bodies.

Schedules of rates

If these are permitted to be incorporated in the contract, in the absence of bills of quantities, then the conditions of contract should make this clear.

Frequently on smaller projects, and in the absence of bills of quantities, the lowest tenderer will be called upon to provide his own schedule of rates. Such a schedule is intended to provide a pricing basis in the event that variations are asked for post-contract.

Progress and programming

Requirements may vary as to whether there is a contractual responsibility for the contractor to produce a programme. It is good practice to call for a programme which may then be used as a means of monitoring actual progress on site.

SO's instructions

Most contracts include the right of the SO to deal with such things as variations and modifications to the works, the issue of explanatory notes including the clarification of possible differences between drawings and specification, the removal of defective work and materials, the opening up of work for inspection if things are covered over prematurely, the use of materials such as sand which may be encountered when forming excavations, and other rights and obligations under the contract.

In some conditions, particularly those used by governmental and similar departments, agencies and commissions, the powers of the SO may be wider, in the public interest, and extend to additional matters such as the hours of working, the extent of overtime working and nightwork, the suspension of the works if deemed necessary, the replacement of workmen and foremen and the execution of emergency work. Invariably when the SO's powers are wider they tend to create additional contractual grounds under which a contractor may claim extra financial reimbursement unless the contractor is in default.

The conditions should stipulate the client's means of redress if a contractor fails to comply with an SO's valid instruction issued under the terms of the contract conditions.

Valuation of SO's instructions

This condition will usually describe in some detail the means by which a contractor is paid for complying with an SO's instruction. The usual order in which such matters are dealt with on the larger contracts is:

1. by measurement and valuation at rates contained in the bills of quantities or in the schedule of rates;
2. by measurement and valuation on a pro rata basis if rates in the bills of quantities or schedule of rates are not strictly relevant;
3. by measurement and valuation at fair rates and prices. This is the means employed when suitable rates and prices cannot be derived from bills of quantities or schedules of rates;
4. by daywork. This is the means of last resort. This cost reimbursement method should only be used if work is physically incapable of measurement or if other very special circumstances apply;
5. conditions creating rights to special payments. This is a complex matter where quantity surveying advice should be sought.

Contracts based on bills of approximate quantities or provisional bills of quantities or schedules of rates

If the contract is based on such documentation then, in essence, the method of valuation and payment will closely follow that described above.

Changes in governmental tax impositions

Some conditions of contract will allow the reimbursement of such increases, including increases in National Insurance contributions. The rationale behind such an entitlement is that neither the contractor nor market forces in general can be said to have any control over governmental decisions of this type.

Setting out the works

Although the designer is responsible for providing such drawn information as is necessary to perform the works, the actual responsibility for taking site levels, setting out and erecting profiles is the contractor's responsibility. On conservation work it is possible that such a condition extends to the taking of measurements so that templates and casts of mouldings and other features may be prepared.

Things to comply with descriptions of materials and workmanship

Such a condition may include the right of the SO to inspect goods off-site and to permit testing. The facility for off-site inspection is particularly important in conservation where there may be the need to inspect stone-bearing quarries, logged timber or standing trees, manu-facturing sources for bricks, terracotta, work being carved in specialist workshops and iron foundries or other places involved with cast iron, cast lead or similar repairs.

Local and other authorities' notices and fees

This is generally a standard clause setting out the responsibilities for the payment of fees for such things as a local authority's building inspector's visits and other costs which are generally unavoidable. In this connection, however, it should be noted that work for the Crown may be exempt from the payment of such fees.

Patent rights

This condition generally places the responsibility onto the contractor to meet any royalties, licence fees or similar expenses if patented or proprietary goods or processes are specified.

Clerk of works/resident engineer

It is customary for the client to reserve the right to appoint a clerk of works and/or resident engineer. If such an appointment is made then the salary and expenses associated with the cost of employing such staff are the client's financial responsibility. The contract documents will usually call upon the contractor to provide suitable on-site offices, toilets, telephone, heating, furniture and cleaning for the clerk of works or other on-site representative.

If complex or extensive restoration or conservation work is involved then it is generally in the client's interests to employ either a full-time or part-time resident representative to carry out the necessary inspec-tion and supervisory duties.

A clerk of works would also be able to closely monitor work per-formed against provisional sums or provisional quantities, is well placed to check any daywork and can receive and issue notices which may be required by the contract.

The design team will normally advise the client on the need for the appointment of a clerk of works or resident engineer well before the constructional work commences on site.

Watching, lighting and protection of the works

In addition to obligations of a general nature which may be referred to in the conditions of contract it is necessary to consider whether con-siderations of a specific nature need to be written into the specification. On conservation work it is not uncommon for works to be taking place in buildings which have valuable paintings or other works of art. This calls for discussions with the client who may wish to arrange for his own security guards, dog handlers and other alarms during the period of the building contract. It is likely that special measures will have to be considered if the works activities increase the threat of theft or vandalism. If special security measures are being taken by the client then a general mention, but not actual details, needs to be provided to the contractors tendering. For example, if electronic or heat-sensing alarms are to be installed then a contractor needs to know that contact with a named individual or telephone extension when entering, leaving or working in areas of high security will be required.

Precautions to prevent nuisance

Nuisance may take several forms in addition to the most obvious causes such as noise and smell. It is possible that nuisance may affect owners, tenants, other occupants, visitors and the public at large. Nuisance can also be caused by the improper pollution of streams and waterways. The responsibility for the prevention of nuisance should be placed on the contractor by means of an appropriate standard condition, but if specific precautions are to be taken then they should be referred to in the specification.

Removal of rubbish

This is generally a standard condition which requires a contractor to keep a site tidy and clean at all times. The requirement should be rigorously enforced particularly if litter or debris is likely to detract from a building and its setting, or if such rubbish is likely to lead to an infestation of vermin.

Apart from a standard condition there may be a particular need to describe in the specification the routes which must be followed when disposing of rubbish and other debris. If the contract documentation is silent on the matter of routes which are to be followed then the contractor is likely to adopt the shortest and easiest routes – a route which may not be in the client's interests.

The removal of rubbish and debris assumes greater importance on historic sites. It may be necessary to specify the frequency of cleaning operations particularly if the premises are open to the public.

Excavation and material arising

Strictly speaking materials removed usually remain in the ownership of the client unless the title is passed onto the contractor by the terms of the contract. The specification should refer to disposals.

On some sites the excavated material may have value. Typical examples would include good quality sand and gravel, stone or other material which could be used as hardcore, or possibly even stone taken from old quarries (where planning approval may be needed for such extraction) which would have a value as a building material either for use on the client's own estate or for sale to others.

Foundations

It is customary to require the contractor to obtain the SO's approval on excavations and trimmed bottoms of excavations before permitting concrete to be poured or before allowing covering over.

Contractor to give notice prior to covering work

Excavated work was dealt with in the preceding paragraph. However in conservation/preservation work there are many other instances when approval must be obtained before a contractor is allowed to cover over. The action and costs which arise following non-compliance should be clearly spelled out in the appropriate condition.

Suspension for frost etc.

Many conservation activities properly have to cease if the weather is so adverse that there is the risk of damage from frost, inclement weather or other similar causes arising. Many conditions of contract give the contractor an entitlement to an authorized extension of time in the contract period if the work has to be suspended because of such adverse weather conditions. To qualify for an extension it is customary for there to be a total suspension of the work or suspension of such a nature that the contract period is at risk. The main effect of granting an extension of time for such circumstances is to create a lengthening of the contract period which then protects the contractor against liquidated damages for the extended period. There is normally no entitlement to extra money if the work has to be suspended for frost and similar natural causes, described in the conditions.

The question of temporary protection which may permit work to proceed in otherwise adverse conditions should be described in the specification. Temporary roofs and disposal of rainwater fall into this category.

Daywork

The contract may permit payment of daywork to a contractor provided all the contract conditions in respect of such entitlement are fulfilled. Daywork is generally the most contentious way of paying for varied work and for stoppages and similar circumstances. Daywork means that payment is on a cost-plus basis and the client, or the SO or clerk of works, have little real control over the hours booked to such activities.

It is stated elsewhere, and is worthy of being repeated, that payment on a daywork basis should only be permitted when all other means of payment, described in the conditions, are unsuitable. Generally, particularly on larger projects, the discretion as to whether or not to permit daywork rests with the quantity surveyor.

Precautions against fire and other risks

This normally places a responsibility on the contractor to comply with statutory regulations which govern the storage of explosives, petrol and other flammable or corrosive products which may be brought onto a site. The conditions should be closely examined to ensure that they provide the basic precautions which are suitable and appropriate for the site involved. Bearing in mind that some old buildings may be particularly vulnerable to fire and other risks then any additional specific precautions which are deemed prudent should be fully described in the specification so that there is no doubt over the contractor's precise responsibilities. It is likely that in some buildings extra fire fighting equipment, such as fire blankets and fire extinguishers, will have to be provided, on a temporary basis, by the contractor. The contract may also place a responsibility on the contractor to have the building and its contents examined by a named individual at the end of each working day and when all other workmen have left the site.

The need for insurances and/or the liability in respect of fire and other risks is normally dealt with under a separate condition.

Damage to the works or other things

A customary requirement is to place the responsibility for damage to the works on the contractor; this responsibility should extend to existing structures. The conditions of contract may or may not require a contractor to cover his liabilities by way of insurance.

Assignment or transfer of contract

A contractor is normally prohibited from assigning or transferring the contract or any part thereof to another, since this would be an attempt to evade any contractual obligations to the client. Assignment which is effectively a total transfer of rights and obligations is not the same as a contractor engaging the services of a nominated or domestic subcontractor to perform part of the works. In the latter case the contractor is responsible for the activities of any sub-contractors.

Date for completion

This, particularly on conservation work, should be of a realistic length to permit the quality of work required. Not all materials needed in conservation work are readily available and time is needed to assemble and properly deploy the various craftsmen for the task in hand. If necessary, clients must be advised of the risks associated with contract periods which are too optimistic.

Extensions of time

Many contracts permit the contractor an authorized extension of time for certain circumstances. By granting a formal extension of time the contractor is protected against liquidated damages being imposed for the period covered by the extended contract period.

Generally the circumstances which may give rise to a legitimate claim for an extension of time will include the need to perform substantially modified or additional work, weather conditions which cause a stoppage in the works, strikes or lock-outs which are beyond the contractor's control, any of the accepted risks and any act or default by the client which causes an over-run.

There is a difference in the philosophical approach to nominated sub-contractors. Standard governmental conditions take the stance that all sub-contractors are the contractual responsibility of the contractor; if he or she needs to seek redress for an overrun by a sub-contractor then it is their right, if they so choose, to make claim against the sub-contractor. The other approach, as in the principal JCT Conditions, is to allow an extension of time to the main contractor when a nominated sub-contractor causes delay. This latter approach weakens the contractual link between contractor and nominated sub-contractor and is the cause of many disputes where the client often ends up as the loser either in terms of time or money, or both.

Some risks may give rights of extra payment to a contractor whereas others do not. As a generalization a contractor may expect reimbursement for those circumstances which are brought about by the action or inaction of the SO or client. Circumstances such as bad weather which causes a stoppage, whilst probably being legitimate grounds for an extension of time, do not qualify for extra payment; this is because it would be manifestly unfair to penalize a client for matters such as continuously heavy rain which may cause stoppages – these are effectively 'Acts of God'.

Phased or sectional completion

Frequently it is necessary to consider whether the works should be completed in one operation or in a series of two or more separate phases. Phasing is particularly likely if the whole or part of an existing building is in occupation or if, as with many listed or historic buildings, the premises are open to the public. It should be noted that total closure can be a serious financial burden to owners when a property relies on the income derived from visitors to help pay for its upkeep.

If phased or sectional completion is required then this must be clearly stated in the contract otherwise a contractor will perform the works in the manner which best suits his own interests and not those of the client. The requirement to hand over separate completed packages of work before being allowed to start on a subsequent phase is often accompanied by separate amounts of liquidated damages for each separate phase.

The partial closure of a building need not be without interest to visitors particularly if they are provided with viewing points. Notices explaining the need for the temporary closure and the nature of the sensitive conservation work involved all create an interest of their own and can be educational.

Liquidated damages

These are pre-determined sums of money which are referred to in a contract and which become payable from the contractor to the client in the event of the contractor overrunning the contract period. It has been previously stated that some circumstances may create an entitlement to an authorized extension of time which has the effect of lengthening the contract period.

The amount included for liquidated damages must be a sum which represents an accurate forecast of the client's real extra expense to which he would be put should the contract not be completed on time. A contractor would be able to challenge in the courts any sum which is effectively a penalty as compared to a reasonable and proper assessment of the client's extra expense for late completion.

Before settling on a sum, or sums in the case of phased completion, to be incorporated in a contract for liquidated damages, it is necessary for the client and his professional advisors to list and value the items of extra expense which would occur in the event of late completion.

Sub-letting

It is a frequent and necessary requirement that the contractor is to obtain the SO's approval before sub-letting any of the works. The client or the SO acting on his behalf should not unreasonably withhold such consent but they will need to satisfy themselves that there will be no lowering of standards or of performance.

Sub-contractors and suppliers

These fall into two principal categories. Firstly there are nominated sub-contractors or nominated suppliers where the SO has the contractual right to select and nominate such firms for the performance of work or the supply of materials. The procedure is for the SO to instruct the contractor to place his official order for the previously selected packages of works and/or supplies with the firm nominated by the SO. Once the contractor has placed his official order with such specialist firms then a contractual relationship has been created between them. The contractor will normally price for profit on all work to be performed by nominated firms; additionally he has the contractual entitlement to the retention of a stipulated cash discount if he pays their accounts promptly. On most projects the main contractor will have to provide specified attendance on such nominated sub-contractors so that they are able to effectively perform their sub-contract tasks. Typical items of attendance which a contractor might have to provide would be the use of standing scaffolding, electric lighting and power, welfare facilities, and other items of a similar but temporary nature which are needed so that the works may proceed.

The second category of sub-contractors or suppliers are known as 'domestic'. Such domestic sub-contractors and suppliers are firms of the contractor's own choosing and in practical terms are regarded as being part of the contractor's own organization. The financial and contractual arrangements between a contractor and his own domestic sub-contractors/suppliers are of no real concern to the SO provided the work is of a satisfactory standard.

There is also a variation on a theme in respect of domestic sub-contractors and this relates to 'named' sub-contractors. The naming process may be incorporated in a specification or bill of quantities by listing out or naming a number of firms with whom a contractor is either permitted or required to select a firm of his own choice, frequently the cheapest, and to employ the chosen firm as a domestic sub-contractor. Named sub-contractors do not enjoy the same contractual status as nominated sub-contractors. The naming process is frequently used as a device to avoid the complicated contractual arrangements which may arise, particularly with the JCT Standard Form of Building Contract 1980 edition, in respect of nominated sub-contractors.

Defects liability period

Most contracts include a maintenance period during which time it is the contractor's responsibility to rectify any faults which are notified to him and which are the result of unsatisfactory work or faulty materials. The defects liability period is generally of six months duration but this period may be varied to suit the project. It is important to remember that some defects will only manifest themselves after the works have been completed and the building occupied. Some defects are more likely to show up in winter months and others during the summer; for this reason there are strong grounds for ensuring that the defects liability period spans at least part of both a winter and a summer period.

Contractor's site supervision

It is highly desirable that there is a competent foreman or agent resident on the site or in attendance at specific periods so that the works are properly supervised by the contractor. Any instruction from the SO should be given direct to the contractor's representative on site and verbal instructions should always be confirmed in writing.

Daily returns

On larger projects, particularly for governmental departments, the contracts will include a condition requiring the contractor to maintain proper records of all workmen employed on site, records of all materials delivered to the site, and a separate record of when the most significant items of plant and equipment are delivered to or removed from the site. Such records are of great help in the event of disputes or claims arising.

Site and other regulations

Any specific or general requirements which a client or the SO requires the contractor to comply with must be stated. Some sites or estates have stringent regulations which may affect a contractor's method of working and, in consequence, will have a bearing on tender prices.

If certain standing regulations can be relaxed for the purpose of the contractor carrying out the works then this should be declared at tender stage so that the benefit is reflected in tender prices.

Replacement of contractor's employees

This is a condition which may enable the SO to order the contractor to remove any unsatisfactory workmen from the site. The requirements are sometimes extended to include supervisors or foremen but the actual condition needs to be examined to determine the SO's precise powers.

Attendance for measurement and provision of information

When work is varied it is essential to have the right to be able to insist on having the contractor or his representative attend so that the varied work may be fully noted and hopefully agreed. Some costs cannot be ascertained without sight of invoices hence the proviso calling for the 'provision of information'.

Prime cost sums

Prime cost sums are not to be confused with prime cost contracts. The latter are dealt with elsewhere.

Prime cost sums, normally denoted by the abbreviation 'PC' are amounts included in bills of quantities or specifications for work to be executed or materials to be provided on the specific instructions and by way of nomination by the SO. At the final settlement of accounts the actual invoice cost, if agreed, is set against the PC sum included in the contract. In the case of contracts incorporating bills of quantities it is also necessary for the quantity surveyor to adjust the contractor's allowance for profit and which will be expressed as a percentage in the bills.

Because nominations tend to lead to or encourage a division of responsibilities between contractor and sub-contractor it is considered good practice to avoid the use of PC sums whenever possible.

Provisional sums

These are amounts included in bills of quantities or specifications for elements of work which, for a variety of reasons, may be incapable of being fully described in detail for pricing by the tenderers. Such sums may conveniently be used when it is known that something will have to be performed under the contract but the precise nature or extent of the work cannot be determined at tender stage. On occasion the nature and extent of such work cannot be ascertained until the work on site has sufficiently advanced and perhaps hidden parts of the structure carefully unpicked to reveal the nature of the remedial task.

A typical example of the use of a provisional sum would be when it is known or suspected that dry rot will be encountered but there is no way of describing, at tender stage, what precisely has to be performed. Once the hidden or previously unknown extent of the rot is discovered then a decision can be taken on the remedial work required. The cost of carrying out the work is then set against the provisional sum included in the contract.

There are many instances of the use of provisional sums and it is a useful device to enable a project to proceed to competition whilst being fair to both client and contractor.

Provisional quantities

As a generalization only contracts incorporating bills of quantities will include provisional quantities.

Provisional quantities are included as part of a contract where the general nature of the work required is known but the extent or quantity of the operations to be performed cannot be determined until work is under way on site. Provisional quantities are commonly used in underpinning, breaking up wholly or partially hidden obstructions, and in carrying out dry rot or similar treatment where it is intended to use the main contractor for such a purpose. In practice there will be many instances of when provisional quantities are appropriate.

The use of provisional quantities is to be preferred to the use of a provisional sum since an agreed basis of payment then exists in the contract. The rates inserted by tenderers against those items which are the subject of provisional quantities will have been the subject of competition and are readily available for use when the actual work performed has been measured and quantified.

Payments on account

Proper cashflow may be regarded properly as the life-blood of the construction industry. Conditions of contract, therefore, generally describe in some detail such matters as the intervals of time between payment entitlement, the right to be paid for both work performed on site and materials properly brought onto the site, and the deduction of retention monies (known as the 'reserve' in some contracts).

Payments on account usually take place at monthly intervals but some contracts may stipulate different periods or payments related to stages of work performed.

The valuation of work performed is usually calculated on a measurement basis and priced out at rates included in the bills of quantities. To this is added the cost of unused materials on site plus the cost of any work performed by nominated sub-contractors and of goods obtained from nominated suppliers. In the absence of a bill of quantities the valuation of work performed is more difficult – here the inclusion of a tender summary may be found useful as an approximate guide to work value. However, in the latter case, since it will be the contractor who will be preparing his own valuation he must be prepared to justify the build-up of his assessment of the amount due to the satisfaction of the SO.

Most contracts will entitle the quantity surveyor or SO to deduct retention from the gross amount otherwise due. This retention is generally expressed as a percentage and the permitted deduction for retention will vary depending on the conditions of contract being used. A frequent retention is 5% or 10% on many contracts in the private sector. In the public sector the general deduction for reserve (reserve being the equivalent of retention) is 3%.

The deduction of retention is a recognition that the valuation of work performed and value of materials delivered to site is, at best, a close assessment of the real value. To attempt to calculate the true value to the nearest pound would generally be a time-wasting and futile exercise since the value of a contract which is making satisfactory progress is likely to increase in value from day to day and depend to some extent on the flow of materials to the site. The retention also provides a 'cushion' to help ensure that a contractor is not overpaid.

Payment after practical completion on site

Most conditions provide that a contractor is entitled to have the value of retention monies reduced by half once the SO has certified practical completion and the client is in a position to enjoy beneficial occupation or the equivalent. At the end of the defects liability period the contractor normally becomes entitled to the release of all retention monies provided he has rectified any defects of which he has been notified.

Certificates

Contracts generally require the issue of an SO's certificate before a contractor is entitled to payment. Such certificates should be honoured by the client and payment made to the contractor either in accordance with the timetable which may be described in the conditions or otherwise within a reasonable time.

Determination of the contract

Determination or the ending of a contract may be invoked by either the client or the contractor subject to what is stated in the conditions. Clearly the determination of a contract is a serious matter and it may be necessary to seek legal advice before invoking such a contractual provision. If the contract is silent on the matter of determination then it is always prudent to obtain legal advice before attempting to bring a contract to an end.

Injury to persons and property

In practice most contractors carry insurance cover by means of a blanket insurance policy which covers them, up to certain financial limits, in the event of them being responsible for the death of or injuries to persons or for loss or damage to the property of others. However, it is prudent to ensure that the particular contract conditions which are being considered as the basis of the contract provide adequate protection to the client and require the contractor to accept liability for and/or insure himself against such risks.

The liability for injury to persons and property is a complex matter and may justify further investigation. However most standard conditions of contract place a heavy responsibility on contractors.

Damage to the highway and other roads
This risk is generally placed on the contractor. However some contracts transfer a certain element of risk and liability onto the client in the event of 'extraordinary traffic' as defined by the Highway Act (England and Wales) or the Road Traffic Act (Scotland).

The risk of possible damage to estate and other private roads usually poses particular problems, especially if there is an element of shared use with others. Certainly roads, bridges and footpaths within the curtilage of an estate are likely to be less robust than those in a public highway. Some estate bridges are not particularly strong and it may be necessary to impose load restrictions. If disputes are to be avoided it is essential to be completely clear in the contract documentation as to the extent of a contractor's liability for damage to access routes. Some contracts may limit a contractor's liability to the making good of any potholes or cracks which may be caused, others may require the roads and footpaths to be completely re-surfaced at the contractor's expense on completion, whilst others may adopt the attitude that some damage is an inevitable consequence of having the work performed and the client will himself arrange for the eventual reinstatement. Clearly these are matters which require careful consideration at tender stage.

Damage to mains, pipes and cables
Here again the responsibility is usually placed on the contractor, who is expected to exercise reasonable care so as to avoid such damage.

Where mains pipes and cables are on an estate then the proposed standard conditions need to be examined to ensure that they give the client the necessary degree of protection against claims for damage. It may be necessary to introduce a supplementary condition or include an appropriate clause in the specification or bills of quantities.

When working within an existing building the contractor should be called upon to protect all existing installations from the effects of his activities. The client should also be asked to what extent, if any, the contractor may make use, on a temporary basis, of an existing installation. The use by a contractor of existing electrical power and lighting may involve the client in extra payment to the supply authority and it may be decided to permit a link into an existing system if the contractor's own meter is provided and the contractor pays for any temporary installation costs and the cost of all electricity consumed. This, and similar considerations, should be taken into account when drafting the specification.

Others employed direct by the client
On occasion the client may need to engage experts to perform certain activities on the site at the same time as the contractor's work is pro-

ceeding. If this is likely then it is essential to stipulate what is to be undertaken by others so that tenderers may take the likely inconvenience into account when preparing their tenders. Without such a provision the client could well be faced with a claim for prolongation or disruption from the contractor if the regular or anticipated progression of his work is in any way affected.

Prolongation and disruption

Many conditions contain a contractual right for a contractor to recover his extra expenses, and possibly other costs, if the action or inaction of the SO or client has caused the contractor to suffer costs which he would not have otherwise incurred. The previous paragraph also described a situation where the actions of others 'employed direct' could lead to similar claims.

Generally matters which are outside the control of the client or SO do not give grounds for a prolongation or disruption claim. This is a complex subject and advice from a quantity surveyor is recommended.

Admission to the site

Any restrictions about admission to a site must be described. A general power may be retained within a contract so that undesirables may be banned from admission.

Passes

These may be required to be issued if work is taking place on a site where admission charges are levied or where particular security measures are in force.

Photographs

If the client wishes to reserve the rights to take photographs then this should be stated. Normally the taking of photographic records of uncovered work and work at various stages of progress is to be encouraged on conservation work. There may be those photographs that have a value to the client and which he may wish to utilize commercially. Alternatively, and frequently in the case of conservation work on truly historic buildings or ancient monuments, there is the probability that an archaeologist, historian or inspector may wish to arrange for independent photographic records to be taken by professional photographers; these photographs then become part of the historic record of the building or monument concerned.

Arbitration

When setting up a new contract the last thing usually contemplated is that a serious dispute may arise. Nevertheless differences do arise on constructional activities when the differences between contractor and client (or his or her agent) cannot be resolved. In these circumstances it may be necessary to refer the dispute to arbitration. Most of the standard conditions of contract include an arbitration clause.

Value added tax (VAT)

It is customary to invite tenders which are exclusive of VAT. Within the UK it is Her Majesty's Customs and Excise who effectively decide whether a construction-related activity is subject or not to VAT. By specifically excluding VAT from tender prices it facilitates adjustments in the VAT rules and regulations which may apply post-contract.

The client must be informed that tenders exclude VAT and advice given as to the likely liability for VAT within the current legislation.

Once a contract has been let it is a contractor's responsibility to be answerable to HM Customs and Excise in respect of VAT.

OTHER MATTERS

Apart from matters which are specifically referred to in the standard or supplementary conditions of contract there is the need to ensure that the specification and/or bills of quantities cover other aspects of the parties' responsibilities which will be applicable to many conservation projects. It was appropriate to cover some of these other aspects when previously considering some of the contract conditions. Other matters which have not been specifically referred to before or which need amplification are considered below.

Drawings

The contract documentation must make it perfectly clear as to which drawings are to be regarded as contract drawings. It is good practice to list out all the drawings, including sketches, used in the preparation of bills of quantities.

It is particularly helpful to tenderers if the pricing documents are accompanied by a drawing which shows such things as access to the site, space to be allocated to the contractor for his own use and for the erection of a compound, and the location of any temporary fencing, hoarding or screens specifically required by the client.

Pollution

A particular and costly hazard associated with some old estates is when ornamental lakes and ponds need to be cleaned out. It may be found that the silt or other material which needs to be dredged or pumped out is toxic requiring removal to special tips. It is always wise to recommend a chemical analysis of such material and to reveal the findings to the tenderers.

Trees and shrubs

Existing trees and shrubs will almost certainly be of significant value within a landscaped setting. Some plantings may be of particularly rare species or of historic interest, whilst others may be the subject of preservation orders. The specification or bills of quantities must describe any protection measures which are to be taken bearing in mind that some specimens will have taken very many years to achieve their present size. A drawing should be available at tender stage showing those trees and shrubs which are to be protected. Having to work carefully around trees may impose a cost penalty.

Temporary works generally

Temporary works usually play a significant part when older buildings and ancient monuments are being repaired or consolidated. A structural engineer will frequently be called upon to advise in respect of those temporary works which involve an element of engineering design.

Since temporary works may be in position for a long period of time it is generally desirable that the major features are made as unobtrusive as possible without sacrificing the purpose for which they are intended.

Shoring of all kinds, scaffolding in its various forms, and temporary roofs and enclosures are all matters which may play a significant part in the total cost of many schemes. It must not be overlooked that temporary roofs may have to carry heavy loads from snowfall. The disposal of rainwater from roofed enclosures must also be allowed for together with any necessary associated drainage.

Hoardings and similar barriers

Temporary hoardings, screens and fencing must be provided, as needed, both to afford security to the works and to protect the public and other persons using or visiting the site where work is to be performed. As previously explained many visitors to historic buildings and ancient monuments may be interested in the work which is taking place and they can be catered for at little expense by the provision of viewing points or panels, and suitable explanatory notices. Some groups may find visits to sites which are undergoing repair or consolidation to be of particular interest.

Scaffolding

Of all the temporary works this is often one of the most important and costly. The type of scaffolding allowed must be such that it will not cause staining to ornamental plasterwork, brick facings or stone elevations and dressings. The design of scaffolding is generally, but not always, a matter which is left to the main contractor and any domestic sub-contractors. On some schemes it is necessary to provide access and inspection scaffolding before a main contractor has been appointed and in such circumstances decisions will have to be taken on the type of scaffolding needed, the loads it is to carry, the means of attachment to the existing building, if permitted, or whether it is to be entirely independent of the existing building.

The design aspect of scaffolding calls for an up-to-date knowledge of current safety legislation and sufficient engineering expertise so that it is fit for the purpose. The possible need to alter and adapt scaffolding during the progress of the works must also be allowed for in the specification.

If the scaffolding is likely to be in position for a long period of time then it is worth obtaining quantity surveying advice as to whether it might be more economic to purchase the scaffolding outright instead of paying hire or rental costs. The rental for scaffolding can be very expensive.

Safeguarding the works, the existing premises and its contents

Injury to persons and property is a likely condition to be found in most conditions of contract but the terms need to be scrutinized to ensure that they cover all of the risks to which a client may be exposed. If there is to be any division of responsibilities between client and contractor then the demarcation must be clearly stated in the specification and/or bills of quantities.

The protection of an existing historic building and its contents must be given the thought it deserves. If the contractor is to provide and maintain temporary protection then it must be fully described. Insofar as contents such as furnishings, paintings and other works of art are concerned it is best if the client accepts responsibility for the removal and safe-guarding of such articles before the contractor starts work on site.

The maintenance of necessary levels of humidity within an existing building can be particularly important because of the effect moisture movement can have on a structure, the finishings and its furnishings. The need to dry out new or replacement construction also presents its own problems because of the frequent increase in moisture vapour levels which may need to be carefully monitored and controlled. If such responsibilities are to be placed on a contractor then the specified requirements must be carefully thought out; there should also be appropriate liaison with curators or others who have a responsibility for a building's contents.

Space for a contractor's own facilities

Offices, workshops, messrooms and other temporary buildings will need to have space allocated so that a contract can be performed effectively. The location of contractors' compounds should be marked on drawings which are issued with the tender documents. In the case of work to prestigious buildings care will need to be exercised over the siting of temporary facilities. If the building is also open to the public then particular care needs to be taken over the separation of the movement of the contractors' workforce, materials and plant away from the general public.

Protected species of animals and plants

Rare and protected species of both animal and plant life may be encountered, particularly on some of the larger and more remote estates. Several of our older ancient monuments form a favourite haunt of endangered species such as bats, whilst other sites may form host to rare plants which, because of their location, are free of some of the modern sprays, herbicides and insecticides which can impoverish our environment. If the existence of rare or protected species is known or suspected then the circumstances should be properly investigated so that their presence may be referred to in the specification. In the case of bats it may be necessary to plan the building operations around their breeding cycle or attempt to arrange for their temporary or permanent removal by the relevant specialist to another suitable location. When rare plants are found to exist then access routes and compounds must be located to avoid the risk of damage. Lack of thought with respect to rare or protected species can bring an otherwise well organized programme to a halt with the consequential financial burdens and frustration which follow.

Name boards and advertising

Name boards may or may not be permitted but advertising is generally banned from sensitive sites. Clients should be asked whether they have any objections to well proportioned and seemly name boards, but it is customary to grant permission to the erection of a well designed and properly signwritten name board carrying the contractor's name and those of the principal sub-contractors. It is also customary to attach to the contractor's name board the separate name boards of the various professional consultants involved – these name boards are normally obtainable in two standards sizes. It is best if the setting out of the overall name board is agreed between the SO and contractor at the first meeting prior to the commencement of activities on site.

Some clients require a brief descriptive narrative of the job description to be displayed on the name board. This helps to create public interest and to assuage concern as to what is taking place.

Contingencies

These are sums of money which need to be budgeted for to meet the cost of the unknown or unexpected. The probability of meeting unforeseen circumstances on large or complex conservation schemes is obviously much greater than on straightforward new building work. Even when a conservation project has been as fully pre-planned as possible it is still necessary to advise the client to budget for an appropriate contingency allowance.

To meet the unforeseen circumstances described above it is normal practice to set aside a specific percentage of the anticipated tender sum to meet these unknown costs. The amount for contingencies is variable but it is recommended that on lump sum projects the total contingency allowances should range between say 6–10%. The lower figure is probably more appropriate to projects for new buildings located on sites where archaeological remains may possibly be encountered. On building conservation projects an allowance of 10% or even more may be justified.

These percentage allowances for contingencies relate to lump sum contracts. If other forms of contract are to be used such as prime cost, contracts based on schedules or rates, or other types of contract which do not incorporate a pre-contract firm price, then the client should be advised to set aside considerably more than 10% for contingencies.

With lump sum contracts it is inadvisable for the contingencies to be fully disclosed in the bills of quantities or specification since they are then all too readily taken to be part of the sum which the client expects to pay. A practice which is to be recommended and which is particularly relevant when bills of quantities are used is to allocate and describe only part of the contingency sum as being a provisional assessment for possible daywork. The manner in which this is dealt with in practice is to include in the bills separate prime cost daywork allowances for labour, materials and plant together with a pricing point against each so that the tenderers may insert their own percentage additions for profit. Provided the definition of prime cost of daywork is fully described in the bills this procedure has the great advantage of making the possible daywork element, inclusive of profit, the subject of competition between the tenderers. An example of a typical provision for daywork is shown in Appendix B.

It is customary for the quantity surveyor and client to agree on that proportion of contingencies which is to be expressed as daywork within the bills of quantities. If it is agreed that one fifth of the total may be allocated to daywork and an appropriate additional allowance also included for archaeological finds (see below) then it follows that the remaining balance of undisclosed contingencies should be kept on reserve by the client.

Archaeological finds

Ancient or historic remains are likely to be found on many heritage sites. The consequences of such antiquities being discovered can cause a total or partial stoppage of the works with consequential disruption and/or prolongation to the contractor. One of the largest conservation organizations within the UK recognizes the distinct possibility of archaeological remains being encountered on its many sites. It accordingly makes special provision for pricing the consequences of such stoppage or delay in the bills of quantities or in a separate tender summary on projects based only on drawings and specification. By including such matters as part of the competition between the tenderers it ensures that the contract includes previously agreed allowances in the event that archaeological finds bring the project to either a total or partial stoppage.

Appendix A includes an example of a suggested insert in a bill of quantities for archaeological finds. However the example given could readily be adapted to those contracts which do not include bills but which are based on drawings and specification.

The example given is an instance of when quantity surveying advice is used to best advantage in what otherwise would prove to be a very difficult contractual issue to resolve. Experience has shown that work priced for at tender stage, being subject to competition, gives a far greater probability of financial benefit to the client. The alternative is to wait for an event to happen and then being faced with the daunting task of attempting to negotiate an amicable and reasonable settlement at post-contract stage. Of all contractual claims those associated with prolongation and disruption are often the most difficult to resolve.

Other circumstances influencing cost

Before concluding this chapter it is appropriate to briefly consider the time of the year, weather, and such things as tidal conditions, all of which influence the cost of works activities. If there is a choice between performing conservation work in favourable rather than adverse conditions then this is likely to lead to a more favourable cost as well as facilitating work of an appropriate standard. Some outside activities cannot be satisfactorily performed in adverse weather conditions particularly during periods of frost and heavy rain. Other sites and locations may include physical barriers such as access only being possible at low or high tide. Other instances occur when delivery of plant and equipment and heavy or bulky materials have to be shipped to otherwise inaccessible locations. If offshore work is involved or work is to take place in river estuaries or other areas affected by tidal conditions, then the fact should be referred to in the specification and consideration given to the inclusion of tide tables in the documentation.

The professional men or women responsible for works of conservation should always attempt to view the proposed activities through the eyes of a contractor. If such a policy is adopted it is likely to lead to tighter, clearer and better contract documentation. It is also likely to provide a better service to the client since a comprehensive consideration of all the factors which are likely to be involved will reduce the likelihood of disputes and claims arising.

PART SEVEN

Grant Aid

Chapter Sixteen

Grant aid

The creation of a building contract for conservation work frequently leads to the question of whether the project will qualify for grant aid. This chapter seeks to deal with much of the background information which will be of interest to professionals and lay people alike.

Towards the end of this book, at Appendix F, will be found references to the principal sources of grant aid or contact points within the UK for obtaining information on financial assistance or advice. The sources of aid or information which are listed include not only those who may be helpful in respect of building conservation work but also those, sometimes on a more local basis, who may be able to assist an enquirer in pursuing other sources of financial assistance or advice in respect of old traditional buildings where a change of use may be contemplated, and where social and economic planning considerations may be deemed to be of equal or greater importance compared to strict conservation related issues.

The subject of grant aid is complex, continues to evolve, and there are rarely any guarantees that financial or other assistance will be forthcoming until appropriate representations have been made and site visits held. With conservation work the quality and nature of the existing building or monument will frequently determine whether financial aid is likely to be a possibility. On occasion, even if a project appears worthy of consideration, the potential applicant may be told that funds are not available, have become exhausted, or that there is a waiting list of other projects which may be deemed equally eligible for grant aid.

Despite this cautionary note, there is certainly nothing to be lost in making preliminary equiries as to the possibility of financial or other assistance. This is particularly so if the building is known to be listed, if it has some particular architectural or historic feature, if it is part of a group of other buildings which collectively contribute to the special quality of a village, town or neighbourhood, or if a scheduled ancient monument or similar structure is involved. Another category which may attract grant aid is that for old industrial buildings which are considered worthy of retention from a national or local standpoint. The state of a building, even if it is very dilapidated, should not deter enquiries about the possibility of financial assistance for restoration work or possibly 'mothballing'. Even if the original source of enquiry is non-productive in terms of an actual offer of grant aid there always remains the probability that a certain amount of limited but free professional advice will have been obtained. Alternatively other possible sources of grant aid may be suggested to the enquirer or applicant.

Property owners may, and frequently do, make their own enquiries as to the possibility of grant aid. However, because of the specialized knowledge required, a property or building owner would be well advised to entrust negotiations to their own professional advisors. There is no real substitute for a detailed knowledge of building construction and an appreciation of how to deal with faults and the most economic methods of repair.

Very often a preliminary enquiry may best be routed through a local authority's conservation officer. Not all local authorities employ conservation officers and, in such a situation, the approach is probably best made via the planning department. At this point, if the building or monument has particular significance it is most likely that the owner will be directed towards one of the national agencies such as English Heritage, Cadw in Wales, Historic Scotland in Scotland, or the Department of the Environment in Northern Ireland.

Other organizations to whom an enquirer may be referred might include the various regional branches of the Rural Development Commission, the Ministry of Agriculture, Fisheries and Food, the Sports Council, and others. However, these latter organizations will generally be found to have rather specific and limited aims. For example, buildings in rural areas which are capable of conversion to light industrial use, the improvement of community centres and putting redundant buildings to new use may all qualify for financial help. Where there are farming interests then grants may be available for the repair of traditional buildings. The creation of sports facilities within redundant buildings is yet another situation which may qualify for financial assistance. The extent of grant aid available for these other types of activities may be regarded, in planning terms, as more in the nature of assistance towards social and economic aims. The level of grant aid from these other bodies towards single projects is unlikely to be comparable in value to that which may be available for conservation related projects from English Heritage, and its equivalents, in other parts of the UK.

The owners of large estates such as the National Trust and the owners or trustees of some of our more noted listed buildings are generally familiar with the procedural requirements and normally make a direct approach to the various national bodies. To many it may come as something of a surprise to learn that the National Trust is the recipient of substantial sums of grant aid. In other instances, such as with Fountains Abbey, the Trust receives the income from visitors and also enjoys the benefit of conservation work being funded elsewhere. The Trust is responsible, in its own right, for a large programme of conservation work and it is pleasing to note that, on occasion, their aims, which reflect the interests of so many, are also helped by grant aid.

Another example of very worthwhile conservation work which is funded, in part by the state, is the essential repair work to many old redundant churches. The Redundant Churches Fund has limited resources but the objective is to get these old buildings, which are often of significant architectural or historic interest, into as sound a state of basic repair as soon as possible compatible with the availability of finance.

Grant aid, when available, is usually in the form of money payable to a building owner or client from one or more of the organizations listed in Appendix F. It needs to be remembered that any financial assistance provided will only be for approved or eligible work. Payment of grant aid is invariably made retrospectively and this is something which the building owner needs to be aware of since, in most instances, he will have a contractual responsibility to pay a contractor within a stipulated time, or at the very least, within a reasonable time of the completion of that part of the project to which the contractor's payment application applies. The payment of grant aid could well follow on several weeks after a building owner has had to pay a contractor. This has important implications for funding and budgetary control by a client.

It is worth noting that on occasion, in respect of eligible proposals only, the grant offer may also include a significant contribution towards professional fees.

The payment of appropriate fees is to encourage the best use of professional expertise in the interests of the actual building or monument involved. It is also helpful from the viewpoint of the grant aiding organization since their own architects, surveyors and engineers are then able to communicate, in a meaningful way, with fellow professionals acting on the client's behalf.

When fees are allowable it should be noted that there is usually an upper limit to the percentage which may be claimed. This and the fact that fees will only be payable in respect of grant eligible activities should be kept in mind when fees are being discussed and negotiated with clients.

Insofar as professional fees are concerned for conservation work, it is most likely that the professions acting on a client's behalf will be architects or building surveyors, quantity surveyors, and less frequently, structural engineers. In the event that a structural engineer is needed then the element of grant eligible fee for such engineering design work, advice or supervision, is customarily required to be absorbed within that element of the fee attributable to the totality of the design and supervisory functions normally performed by an architect or building surveyor. There is logic in such an arrangement or requirement since the involvement of a structural engineer will reduce the input and professional responsibility of the architect or building surveyor. There is no such blurring of professional responsibility in the case of the quantity surveyor. Provided the total fees for all the professional disciplines involved do not exceed the maximum stipulated by the grant aiding organization then the client need not budget for such expenditure in respect of grant eligible work. Fees in respect of non-eligible work and excess fees which exceed the maximum allowed by those offering grant aid will have to be met in full by the client.

Instances of when an architect, building surveyor or quantity surveyor need to be engaged to look after a client's interests are generally fairly obvious. Anything which involves design work, the recognition and interpretation of faults, and the specifying and supervision of the remedial or restoration work recognisably falls to the lot of the architect or building surveyor. On complex or larger value schemes the financial and contractual issues involved will be particularly important and this is when the services of a quantity surveyor are really essential.

The question of whether or not a structural engineer needs to be appointed is more particularly related to the type of conservation work involved and whether the architect or building surveyor possesses the necessary degree of professional expertise. Occasions when a structural engineer should be appointed will include heavy masonry structures, complex timber framed buildings, and cast iron or similar structures requiring engineering knowledge and experience.

There are times when assistance may be offered to an applicant by means other than grant aid. Some organizations may be prepared to offer loans, sometimes on advantageous terms, when they are unable to offer direct payments which effectively constitute a gift. On occasion, and rather infrequently, a grant applicant may be offered the services of craftsmen employed direct by the grant aiding body. These services may be provided either free or on other terms depending on the circumstances and the availability of the directly employed labour to perform the work.

Grant aid is rarely an entitlement as of right. The funding, as explained elsewhere, comes principally, but not exclusively, from the Government or local authority domain.

The governmental organizations which are listed in Appendix F have the responsibility of allocating funds made available to them from the public purse; they also have the responsibility and difficult task of making policy decisions on how the limited funds are to be distributed, and for deciding those types or categories of buildings, structures and monuments which may be regarded as grant eligible. Unfortunately the funds available by way of grant-in-aid or by direct transfer from Her Majesty's Treasury are never enough to enable the grant aid sponsoring organizations to fulfill all the demands made upon them.

To perhaps explain why many applicants will be disappointed that their application has been unsuccessful or deferred, it is a salutary illustration of the extent of the problem to record that in 1989/90 there existed, in England alone, well over 400 000 listed buildings graded I, II* and II, about 13 000 scheduled ancient monuments (a figure which is expected to increase significantly by the year 2000) and about 7000 conservation areas frequently located in or near the centres of historic towns.

Grant aid from local authorities is also effectively funded from the public domain and therefore limited by constraints resembling those which are applicable to the funding from central government. The medium by which such local authority money is made available comes either from monies raised by way of the community charge, or rates, or from financial assistance rendered direct to a local authority from central government. In any event the money raised for grant aid (and the many other needs of a local authority) effectively comes from the tax-payer or from those who have to contribute towards local taxes through the community charge or rates.

In addition to the possibility of grant aid from a governmental department or a local authority there are various private organizations which may be prepared to contribute towards the cost of conservation work. Obviously the funding available from the private sector is much less than that available from central or local government agencies. Nevertheless private funding is worth considering and some large organizations may be prepared to consider making contributions by way of sponsorship when their name may be associated with the proposed conservation work and possibly displayed in advertising or promotional material. Obviously advertising and similar activities raise the question of what constitutes good or bad taste, and it is something which needs to be explored very carefully before accepting sponsorship from such a source.

The level of grant aid which will be available from all the sources previously referred to can never be guaranteed from one year to the next. Insofar as public funding is concerned there is a finite sum available. This is likely to vary depending on political considerations and on the general health of the economy. In the case of funding from the private sector much will depend on the profitability and fluctuating fortunes of commercial concerns, the need to account to shareholders and, not least, the general level of activity on the Stock Exchange. 'Bull' and 'bearish' conditions on the latter will certainly influence investment decisions made by commercial concerns.

The real purpose of grant aid needs to be kept in mind. It is not there simply to provide a free hand-out without an underlying aim or purpose. It is there to help towards maintaining a nation's stock, usually a limited and therefore precious stock, of historic buildings and heritage sites. These buildings and ancient remains are very much part of our heritage which it is to be hoped can be passed on to future generations. If neglected they could well become lost for ever.

The UK is particularly fortunate in the number of listed buildings, scheduled ancient monuments, archaeological remains and other old structures still remaining. All of these testify to the richness of our inheritance and help to serve in the projection of our own national identity. Elsewhere in the world other countries have their own old buildings and ancient remains which equally serve to provide a pointer to their own past and present national identity. If, by means of grant aid or the equivalent, any nation can help to protect part of its often fragile and very vulnerable built inheritance then not only the present but future generations will almost certainly regard the investment as truly worthwhile. The giving of grant aid for conservation work is probably one of the most significant and tangible statements we can make about our responsibilities to the future as well as to the past.

In the context of grant aid it needs to be remembered that many of our old buildings and ancient remains are in a fragile condition simply because of the passage of time, sometimes through neglect, on occasion through mining subsidence or coastal erosion, and more recently through the corrosive effects of fumes emitted from industrial processes and motor vehicles and the consequences of acid rain.

When a property is in the care or guardianship of the state then the responsibility for the essential upkeep can be readily identified. However, many of our best and most noted historic buildings and ancient monuments, including industrial and agricultural buildings, old bridges, town houses, more humble but noteworthy village dwellings, and groups or terraces of houses in conservation areas or in areas specifically designated as being in need of comprehensive repair and restoration, have to be maintained by private owners or local authorities. Some owners are sufficiently well placed financially that they can afford to properly care for what they own. Other owners, whilst caring, are less well placed financially. In the latter instance the necessary cost of properly maintaining or restoring a building or monument which probably provides enjoyment to others or which may truly be regarded as part of our heritage, becomes a financial burden which the owners may find difficult or impossible to shoulder. At the other extreme are those owners who do not really care about their property and would have little or no compunction in letting their buildings or structures fall into a state of total disrepair leading possibly to total collapse. These deliberately neglected properties are becoming increasingly referred to as 'buildings at risk'. However other 'buildings at risk' are not caused through deliberate neglect but arise as a result of their owners lacking sufficient funds to be able to carry out the necessary and often expensive upkeep. 'Buildings at risk' now constitute a special category which may attract grant aid or even direct action by such a body as English Heritage or a local authority obtaining permission to enter upon land not in their ownership so as to effect the minimum essential repairs which will halt the deterioration in the 'at risk' property. The cost of this intervention may be recoverable, either in whole or in part, from the owner.

When considering grant aid, even for appropriate buildings and meritorious proposals, it needs to be remembered that financial assistance will be limited to work of an approved type. Such approved activities which may attract grant are known as 'eligible works'. As a generalization, attempts to 'improve' a historic building or perhaps the incorporation of upgraded, new or additional facilities to meet a client's requirements or a change of use are unlikely to meet with financial support from the principal grant organizations operating in the conservation field. This restriction, however, may not be applicable to those organizations offering grant aid for purposes other than true conservation. It is in a client's interests, therefore, that a professional advisor considers all likely avenues of grant aid to suit a proposed scheme.

It has already been stated that the amount of funding available for grant aid is finite. From this it follows that an applicant needs to be aware that grant aid is variable and discretionary. Indeed it is not unusual for funding of new projects to have to be declined or deferred part-way through the sponsor's financial year simply because the demand exceeds the availability of funding.

Other important considerations which have to be addressed by a sponsor when considering the extent, if any, of grant aid are:

- the worthiness of the building, groups of buildings, or monument;
- the ability of the owner or owners to pay for the cost of the necessary conservation work.

It is a fact that some of the most noteworthy buildings and estates are in the ownership of extremely wealthy individuals or organizations. Historically those with the greatest wealth have been able to acquire or inherit much of the best of our old buildings, historic houses or landscaped estates. However a past record of wealth within a family does not necessarily mean that the present owners are in the same fortunate financial position. It is frequently necessary, therefore, to devise a method of means testing those applying for grant aid. Bearing in mind the limited funds available, most of which is from the public purse, it does not seem unreasonable to call for evidence of the ability, or inability, to fund extensive conservation work.

There has been a measure of criticism, sometimes seemingly well founded, that grant aid has not always been directed towards those with the greatest need. It is probable that means testing or the establishment of the ability to pay will play a bigger role in the future.

When a sponsor issues an offer of financial assistance it is customary to attach conditions to any grant aid which may be accepted. Typical conditions will include a stipulation to the effect that:

- the project must be handled and supervised by an appropriately qualified building professional;
- competitive tenders must be obtained (and submitted to the sponsor for scrutiny);
- the organization making the grant offer will require the involvement of its own professional staff in the assessment of proposals and in ensuring that all grant eligible work is performed in a satisfactory manner;
- materials used are of appropriate types;
- workmanship is of an approved standard;
- the building owner is responsible for raising all other finance;
- grant aid will only be paid in proportion to the amount of eligible work actually performed;
- grant aid will not be paid until the work has been inspected and approved;
- the amount on offer may not be subject to increases unless there are

exceptional circumstances which have received the prior approval of the sponsor;

- in the event of the work being reduced in scope there will be a corresponding reduction in the amount of grant aid;
- final accounts will have to be properly prepared and submitted for approval and scrutiny by the sponsor;
- the offer must be taken up within a stipulated time and expended within a given period.

These are just typical examples of some of the conditions which may be attached to an offer. Particular site and contractual circumstances will probably also involve the imposition of particular conditions; some of these are described below.

One unnecessarily frequent problem encountered with applications is the proposal or suggestion that the works can only be performed on the basis of prime cost. When one considers that English Heritage, with responsibilities for some 400 historic buildings and ancient monuments of its own, rarely if ever resorts to prime cost contracts, then it is an indication of the lack of thought and design input by some professionals responsible for advising clients of the best and most appropriate contractual arrangement. A similar unsympathetic attitude to prime cost is also likely to be displayed by those building professionals responsible for the upkeep of the many hundreds of other historic buildings and monuments in the care of the state which are scattered throughout the UK and elsewhere. This leads to the need for another cautionary note. If an application is based on prime cost then it is probable that the request may be subjected to particular scrutiny and possibly by the setting of cash limits or other precautionary means of protecting the sponsor's limited funds. The overall effect of this might well be against the building owner's interests in obtaining the maximum financial assistance.

Sometimes the building or monument which is the subject of an application is of such national or other importance, perhaps for a variety of reasons, that the level of grant aid is commensurately higher than usual. When financial assistance comes from public funds it is frequently a requirement that grant aid is conditional on future access being provided to the general public on an agreed basis. The right of public access is likely to be negotiable but there is a presumption that the higher the level of grant the greater should be the availability of access for the general public. Whether this access should be free or chargeable and the time of year and possible opening hours to the public are all matters which will involve negotiation.

Other buildings, perhaps less humble in themselves but possibly part of a conservation area or town scheme may be awarded particularly high levels of financial assistance. In such situations, the grant offer may well include a condition that the property is not to be sold until the expiry of a stipulated number of years. Again this is an instance of a sensible precaution to help protect the public interest. Without such a restriction public money could well be expended to repair or upgrade a property only to find that, once the work is completed, an owner promptly sells and thereby derives a quick profit from publicly funded activities.

On occasion the situation arises where an organization such as English Heritage undertakes to fund the totality of essential conservation work although the property is not in their direct care or guardianship. This situation, although uncommon, leads to the grant aiding body acting as the authority or employer and entering into a contractual relationship with a contractor for the performance of the necessary works. Here it is essential that the grant aiding body enters into a licence or formal agreement with the building or site owner whereby it is agreed that the grant aiding body including its agents, servants and others, also contractors, may enter upon the land and take temporary possession of the existing building so that the necessary works, as described in the licence, may be allowed to proceed.

It has to be said that not all licences are drafted with the care they deserve and by those with professional experience of building activities. It is essential for the professionals involved in works activities which are taking place on land owned by others to take particular care and to ensure that the terms of the licences are subjected to appropriate scrutiny by those responsible for preparing the tender documents. It is also good practice to either incorporate a copy of the licence within the tender documents or to include in the tender documentation a summary of the principal conditions. By following such a practice the licence information will subsequently become part of the building contract. This will avoid any confusion over things such as ownership, rights of access, working hours, limitations on the use of the building, advertising rights, use of services and therefore possibly payment, and other considerations. These are all important matters which a contractor needs to know when he is preparing a tender offer.

An illustration of the need to check licences very carefully is well exemplified by the following example. In this instance a draft licence had been agreed which purported or indeed did allow the grant aiding body's contractor to have the right of entry to the land and to use an old medieval barn for the purpose of essential building repairs. What the licence also included was the owner's right to continue to use the barn for the storage of his own agricultural equipment and machinery, the entitlement to use the barn for his chickens, and the right to also make use of the barn during the lambing season. If this had not been resolved prior to tendering and contract, and in this instance by the quantity surveyor calling for a sight of the original licence and the agreement of an amended licence, then the frustration of the owner farmer, the disruption of the works to the contractor, and the financial claims which would almost certainly have been lodged against the employing authority can well be imagined.

Within the larger grant aiding organizations it is customary to seek in-house professional quantity surveying advice on the greater value or more complex conservation projects. The types of scheme which are most likely to receive detailed scrutiny are those where the potential building contract is of a substantial value, on complex projects calling for a financial analysis of the project, on proposals which include a mixture of possible grant eligible conservation work within the same contract as new activities which do not qualify for grant aid, on proposals where the stated intention is to perform the work on a cost-plus or prime cost basis, and on those projects where the applicant is himself a builder, developer or equivalent and which, for convenience, are referred to as 'developer' schemes.

In many respects the type of application which is likely to present the greatest difficulty for a grant aiding organization is that for 'developer' schemes. This is because the proposal may frequently lack a proper element of true competition and hence raise doubts over whether the proposal really gives the best value for money in terms of public accountability.

As indicated above, applications for grant aid from developers or the equivalent, particularly when they own or have a financial interest in the property, differ from other grant applications in one very important aspect: this is the profit element.

With non-developer schemes there will usually have been the stated intention to invite proper competitive tenders from a number of suitable firms. It therefore follows that the non-developer applicant does not profit directly from an outside contractor's own allowances for trading on-costs and profit. With a 'developer' scheme or self-build proposal things are likely to be considerably different from the normal application insofar as overheads and profit are concerned.

In the case of a 'developer' proposal or a self-build application there is a distinct possibility that the applicant will already be involved in other or similar trading operations; some or all of which may include operational on-costs or other trading overheads. In these circumstances it is possible that he will be asked to provide evidence that his grant aid application excludes operational costs which would have been incurred in respect of his business as a whole. Similarly an applicant for grant aid should not expect to make a direct financial profit out of relatively scarce publicly funded money which is intended to help conserve or protect our built inheritance. For these reasons a 'developer' is likely to be asked to show or prove that his grant aid application excludes overheads and profit. If however it can be shown that the grant eligible work attracts certain on-costs or preliminaries which are peculiar to the project, and which are not covered by other trading operations elsewhere, then consideration is more likely to be given to the admission of such special costs as part of a grant aid offer.

With all grant applications the onus is on the applicant, or his professional advisors, to provide all necessary information and price build-ups to enable a proper professional assessment to be made of all aspects of the application. It is to be expected that the information called for will include drawings and specifications to show the full extent of the proposed work, itemized priced schedules of work for the smaller scheme, bills of quantities for the larger or more complex project, evidence of sufficient competitive tendering including the full tendering results, and most importantly, an analysis of grant eligible and non-eligible activities when a building owner combines in a single 'mixed' contract elements of both new work and conservation activities. In this latter case it is the responsibility of the grant applicant's professional advisors to annotate the specification and bills of quantities to indicate the claimed for grant eligible items. When preliminaries are priced in either a bill of quantities or a priced schedule of works then these will need to be apportioned on a fair and reasonable basis between eligible and non-eligible items in a 'mixed' scheme. As previously explained a 'mixed' scheme is one which incorporates conservation work which attracts grant aid (i.e. eligible work) and those other activities which are probably, and perhaps very sensibly, included in the same contract, but which are, by their nature, improvements, extensions or alterations to suit a client's requirements rather than the true conservation or consolidation of an existing standing historic building or monument.

On occasion, particularly with 'developer' or self-build applicants, they may advance the argument that because they are not in the normal competitive situation they are unable, or unwilling, to produce the full documentation by way of priced schedules of work or priced bills of quantities which would be required from other applicants. In reality developers usually have the ability or resources to be able to substantiate their estimates in a meaningful way if they so wish. Self-build owners are also at liberty to call upon outside professional advice to help with the compilation of costed proposals. However, the submission of any application which is not supported by truly competitive tenders may well lead to unavoidable delay because of the additional in-house professional involvement by the grant aiding organization in researching, analysing and costing these more difficult applications. Even after such investigation there is no guarantee that the anticipated level of grant aid will be made available to an applicant. If an applicant is unable to substantiate his figures or appears to have introduced an element of cost which appears to be higher than it should be then it is possible that the grant offer finally made will have been scaled down to what is deemed to be a more appropriate or competitive figure.

Some self-build individuals and others may seek to justify an application for grant aid on the basis that work will only be charged and claimed for on a prime cost or cost-plus basis. Such an approach is unlikely to meet with much enthusiasm by the professionals called upon to examine the case since financial appraisal and a value for money assessment is extremely difficult. It could well result in the scheme being subjected to a tighter financial limit and the imposition of more onerous conditions than would otherwise be the case. The soundness of professional advice could well also be called into question if, in the event, a prime cost contract has to be abandoned before completion simply because a client's funds have been exhausted by this cost-plus method of proceeding.

Those grant aid applications which are likely to attract a particularly high percentage of financial assistance may also expect to be subjected to a more rigorous scrutiny. The reasons for this are not difficult to understand. If the grantor has a greater stake in the project then it follows that the grantee is less likely to be concerned about the financial and contractual soundness of the scheme as a whole since he is personally less exposed to financial risk.

The question of contingencies is also frequently raised in connection with grant aid. The short answer is that contingencies or a 'float' to meet deficiencies, shortcomings or just the plain unknowns in respect of design or specification matters will generally be excluded from grant aid. The sensible approach for problematical circumstances is to include for them by way of provisional quantities (if a bill of quantities is used) or by way of realistic provisional sums in a specification or bill of quantities. It is prudent for the applicant's professional advisors to draw attention to these problematical parts of a project when submitting a formal application for grant aid. It is possible that alternative means of contracting, as described in this book, may be recommended.

Any applicant for grant aid, particularly on the larger or more complex projects, is well advised to employ his own professional quantity surveyor. Such an individual or firm with past experience and a proven track-record in conservation work and grant aid will be able to help steer a client through what may appear to him to be something of a minefield. An experienced quantity surveyor will be familiar with all the many ways and means of letting building conservation contracts which are described in this book. Such an individual or firm will also readily appreciate the need for comprehensive documentation, competitive tenders from suitable contractors, soundly based contracts which will leave the client free from unnecessary worry and claims, an ability to identify in conjunction with a client's other professional advisors the distinction between grant eligible and non-eligible work, and an ability to talk the same language and thereby ease or hasten a grant application through the organization which is the possible source of grant aid. In reality the benefits derived by a client will often far outweight the professional quantity surveying fees involved. This is particularly true if, as is often the case, the grant aiding organization is prepared to fund reasonable professional fees for such a service.

The applicant or his professional advisors should be aware that approval to grant aid is not made retrospectively. It is vital, therefore, to allow sufficient time for all grant negotiations to take place before actually committing expenditure by way of a binding building contract.

Programmes of activities need to be drafted accordingly since it is most likely that the potential sponsor or grant aiding body will require an architect or building surveyor and possibly also an inspector or archaeologist to be sent to the proposed site in order to determine the merits of the existing building or structure and to discuss, if applicable, the planned programme of repairs or consolidation which the owner has in mind.

Although this book is directed at building conservation work it is worth bearing in mind that grant aid may well be available which is aimed more specifically at social or economic considerations. For example, particularly in rural or deprived urban areas, the interest and therefore the emphasis of the local planning authority may be directed more on the avoidance of depopulation, a desire to avoid the loss of local amenities and services, and a wish to preserve a desirable mix in the different age groups, and in the socio/economic balance in the area or region concerned. These are very important planning issues which should be kept in mind as well as a proper regard for the conservation issues associated with old buildings.

Sometimes a combination of grants from more than one source may be available. On other occasions the receipt of grant aid from an organization may preclude or limit the availability of financial assistance from another body. It is, therefore, always well worthwhile investigating to see whether grant aid may be available to help with the cost not only of historic building repairs but also to ascertain whether financial assistance, either by way of grant or loan, may be available from other sources to help with associated new work or alterations.

In addition to the organizations named in Appendix F as being possible sources of grant aid or as contact points for further advice, there also exist those other organizations which may be prepared to offer financial assistance. Others who could be contacted, and who have previously been referred to, might include the Sports Council, housing corporations, the Department of Trade and Industry, the Department of Employment, and others who, whilst not operating or supporting activities in the conservation field, may be able to offer advice or even a measure of financial assistance if a proposal, other than the conservation aspect of a project, meets their own criteria.

When contemplating work to old buildings, other historic structures and ancient remains it should be remembered that grant aid is not merely limited to operations within the UK. Other countries operate schemes of financial assistance, sometimes through their taxation system, which is likely to be of benefit to owners on virtually a world-wide basis. With the creation of the European Common Market it is likely that financial assistance for eligible projects will become increasingly available to help organizations and individuals whose country is a member state of the European Community. The United Nations, through UNESCO or its other specialized sponsoring bodies, is also likely to play an increasingly greater role in helping to foster both heritage conservation and socio–economic schemes which may be of help to an owner.

Increasingly the reader will need to develop an awareness of all the likely evolving schemes of grant aid. Inevitably the financial assistance which is available will tend to fluctuate with the passage of time particularly for economic and political reasons. One of the most important changes in conservation grants is that, from 1991, extra UK governmental funding is to be provided for repairs to cathedrals. For far too long cathedrals have been totally dependent on the success of a variety of differently funded public appeals to help with their hugely expensive and badly needed repairs. Some of this public funding has been extremely controversial. Some cathedrals, particularly the better known and more frequently visited, have been very successful in raising their own funds; whilst others, particularly those less in the public eye or more distant from a wealth creating population or away from the tourist route have experienced the greatest difficulty in being able to finance even the barest minimum of care to these usually great and monumental works of art.

Parts of the world are now so overcrowded that there is a real threat to the retention of that which is best or that which is most deserving of protection to indicate to future generations the source of their own nation's heritage. Communication between different parts of the world and between adjoining countries is getting better by the day. Education and understanding is spreading. All of these things, and more, will therefore have a profound effect on the extent and value of financial assistance or economic aid which is likely to be available in the future.

PART EIGHT

Appendices

Appendix A

Archaeological finds:
cessation of work

Chapter 15, page 95 already includes a reference to archaeological finds. The types of finds which may be encountered are many and varied. The rather obvious example is if excavations reveal previously unknown archaeological remains. Above ground the opening up of an old building may disclose previously unknown features of significant archaeological, historic or other interest. Another category of discovery is that of old wall paintings. Yet another type of find might include historic graffiti.

An examination of most conditions of contract will reveal that many, particularly those intended for the larger project, will include a clause or condition specifically referring to fossils, antiquities and other objects of interest or value which may be encountered.

The relevant clause or condition will usually state that upon discovery of such finds or remains the action to be taken will comply with the following requirements:

- the archaeological or other find should not be disturbed;
- work should cease which would endanger the objects or articles found;
- the SO is to be informed of such a discovery.

The consequences of the SO or architect being informed of such a discovery is that he or she will call in an archaeologist, historian, conservator or other expert to decide upon the merit of the discovery and what action is most appropriate. It must be recognised that the discovery of archaeological remains or other antiquities will result in a varying degree of disruption to the contractor. If alternative work can be found on site for the workmen involved then the disruption will be minimal and any standing time might possibly be paid for on a daywork basis. If the discovery results in part of the works having to stop then the additional cost will only be related to part of the total workforce on site. On a confined site or if the discovery is particularly large then there may be a total cessation of work. In the latter case the financial consequences are much greater for a contractor. On occasion it is also possible that interesting discoveries will be made on more than one occasion on the same site.

An archaeological finds pricing arrangement for inclusion in a bill of quantities for a privately funded but grant aided project on a sensitive site is outlined below. In this instance the conditions of contract quoted are related to the JCT Standard Form of Building Contract 1980 Edition, Private With Quantities, but similar provisions would be applicable to projects based on other conditions such as Form GC/ Works/1, Edition 2 September 1977; the ACA Form of Building Agreement 1982, Second Edition 1984; and the ICE Conditions of Contract, Fifth Edition (re-printed 1986).

Even when building conservation projects do not include bills of quantities it is good practice to include a similar pricing document to that shown. It may then form part of a tender summary as issued to the tenderers. Subsequently it will become a contract document with the firm whose tender is accepted.

The inclusion of a pricing document for archaeological finds is equally applicable to contracts for new buildings located on ancient sites as it is for building conservation projects to existing structures.

In the example which is given it will be seen that provision is made for:

- cessation of a part of the works;
- cessation of the whole of the works.

'When preparing the archaeological finds documentation it is necessary to consider both circumstances. The design team, usually acting on the initiative of the quantity surveyor, should assess the risk of partial or total cessation or both. In the case of partial cessation it will be necessary to consider the number and type of craftsmen or labourers who could be affected – this will vary from job to job and will be dependent on which parts of a project are at risk of encountering unknown remains. The cessation of the whole of the works is a much more serious matter. In the example shown it has been assumed that the total stoppage will be for not more than three consecutive working days. This total cessation is based on an assumption of the time needed to call in an expert, for the finds to be examined and for a decision to be taken about the resumption of work.

When considering the cessation of the whole of the works it is considered reasonable for a tenderer to be able to assess his extra expense for a period of up to three days and be paid for the cessation on a daily basis. If however the cessation of the works becomes longer in duration then the stoppage may cause a contractor extra expense which cannot be reasonably anticipated and which is more properly dealt with under the conditions of contract which relate to prolongation and disruption. Protracted delays and disruption will almost certainly involve complex negotiations between the contractor and quantity surveyor. However, by incorporating a pricing mechanism on the basis of the example in this Appendix, it is likely that many of the problems associated with the most common stoppages will be catered for.

The question of encountering unknown remains also needs to be considered in the context of the overall initial funding and budgetary control. If there is the probability of archaeological or other remains being encountered then the financial provision for 'Archaeological finds – cessation of work' should reasonably be considered as part of a client's enhanced contingencies fund and budgeted for accordingly. In the event that the possibility of coming across antiquities or other finds is considered remote then it should be considered as coming out of the normal contingency allowance.

Item	Job title: Archaeological finds: cessation of work (all provisional)	Bill 1 – archaeological finds: cessation of work (all provisional)	
		£	p
	Action to be taken upon the discovery of fossils, antiquities, and other objects of interest or value, together with schedule of items to cover reimbursement of direct loss and/or expense in the event of consequent interruption and stoppage of the works		
A	See Condition 34 of the Form of Contract hereinbefore referred to.		
B	The Tenderer should insert below the rates he requires to cover costs resulting from interruptions or stoppages of work arising as a direct result of his compliance with the foregoing Condition.		

Job title: Bill 1 – archaeological
                                              finds: cessation of
                                              work (all provisional)

Item		£	p

*Action to be taken upon the
discovery of fossils, antiquities,
and other objects of interest or
value, etc. (cont'd)*

C   Reimbursement will initially be for
a period not exceeding two hours
provided that upon discovery of
fossils, antiquities, and other
objects of interest or value, this
fact is immediately reported to the
Architect. Should the cessation of
work be of longer duration and
unless otherwise instructed by the
Architect, the Contractor shall use
his best endeavours to re-deploy
his labour and plant elsewhere on
the site.

D   The decision as to whether the
Works shall remain suspended in
whole or in part shall rest with the
Architect. Any cessation exceeding
two hours must be specifically
ordered by the Architect who shall
determine the extent and number
of men and/or items of plant
involved.

E   In the event of the Architect
deciding that any cessation will
exceed three working days then
any direct loss and/or expense
arising from such cessation shall
be ascertained by the Architect or
Quantity Surveyor in accordance
with Condition 34.3 without
reference to the rates inserted
below.

Job title:

Item		£	p
	Action to be taken upon the discovery of fossils, antiquities, and other objects of interest or value, etc. (cont'd)		
F	Reimbursement will only be made for the net time recorded and certified by the Architect or by the Clerk of Works when so empowered by the Architect in accordance with Condition 12.		
G	The rates for cessation of part of the Works (related to craftsmen and labourers who have had to cease working) or for the whole of the Works shall be fully comprehensive to include all charges in respect of labour including bonus, insurances, holidays and the like and, in addition, the cost of hand tools (including those power operated), the cost of working supervisors or chargemen, any wastage of materials, disruption, time lost in demobilisation and in remobilisation after the order to recommence, all preliminary costs and charges, overheads and profit and all other liabilities and obligations whatsoever except as stated at H below.		
H	The rates are to EXCLUDE:–		
	(i) mechanically operated plant which is affected by the		

Job title: Bill 1 – archaeological
                                              finds: cessation of
                                              work (all provisional)

Item			£	p

Action to be taken upon the discovery of fossils, antiquities, and other objects of interest or value, etc. (cont'd)

cessation and for which idle time will be calculated and reimbursed at fair rates and prices having regard to the non-operation of the plant;

(ii) any increases or decreases which are subject to adjustment for VAT under Condition 15 including the Supplemental Provisions (the VAT Agreement).

Schedule of items (all provisional)

Cessation of a Part of the Works

For a period not exceeding 8 hours in total in any one working day

I	Craftsman	. . . . . . hours*	£†	
J	Labourer	. . . . . . hours*	£†	

Cessation of the Whole of the Works

For a period not exceeding three consecutive working days

K	Whole of the Works Working Days‡	£†	

Idle mechanically operated plant

L   Include the Provisional Sum of £. . . . . . for idle mechanically operated plant as described at Item H(i) on Page 121.

Lump Sum to be assessed by Quantity Surveyor and included here

(End of· ALL PROVISIONAL)

To Collection   £

* Assessment of number of hours to be inserted by the Quantity Surveyor (after discussion with the Architect).
† Rates to be inserted by Tenderer.
‡ Assessment of number of days, which may include for more than one occurrence, but not to exceed three consecutive working days for any one event – to be inserted by the Quantity Surveyor after discussion with the Architect.

Job title: Bill 1 – archaeological
                                             finds: cessation of
                                             work (all provisional)

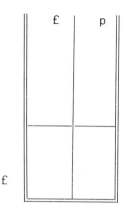

COLLECTION   £   p

From Page .119 .

From   "   .120 .

From   "   .121 .

From   "   .122 .

Archaeological finds:
cessation of work (all provisional)
Carried to Bill 1 Summary
(or Main Summary)   £

Appendix B

Daywork

References to daywork appear at a number of different pages in this book. This includes Chapter 15 pages 79 and 80. Chapter 8 which refers to Daywork Term Contracts is also relevant.

Chapter 15, page 94 (see under 'Contingencies') includes the recommendation that in lump sum contracts it is good practice to include within the tender sum a proportion of the total contingency element by way of daywork. The purpose of including a pricing allowance for daywork is to ensure that excessive daywork rates are not quoted. If the practice is adopted, which is illustrated below, then it is far more likely that a tenderer's allowance for daywork will be fair and reasonable. This is because if a significant part of the total tender sum (say 2% of the anticipated total cost) is allocated to daywork, then the tenderers are on notice that an excess allowance in this part of the tender build-up could lead to the loss of a contract. Sometimes contracts are won or lost by small margins and a contractor's estimator will, with this method, be well aware of the significance of the need to price daywork in a realistic manner.

Most conditions of contract permit payment by way of daywork only if certain circumstances are satisfied. The conditions will normally state that daywork will only be accepted as a basis for payment when work cannot be properly valued by measurement and valuation or the equivalent. It is also customary for the quantity surveyor to rule on whether varied or additional activities are to be paid for on a daywork basis.

In the case of labour in daywork there are two principal methods of obtaining prices. The first method, most frequently adopted in JCT types of contract, requires tenderers to quote a percentage addition to cover their own incidental costs, overheads and profit. This is a perfectly satisfactory method but leaves the calculation of the actual hourly rates for labour to be determined and agreed at the post-contract stage. The other method of obtaining prices for labour in daywork, as adopted by most governmental organizations, is to require the tenderers to quote all inclusive hourly rates for the different types of craftsmen and labourers who are likely to be employed on daywork. With this method the tenderers are able to incorporate their own particular trading circumstances into the quoted hourly rates; such rates are also subject to adjustment to reflect increases which arise because of the passage of time – this is affected by the application of the updating provisions which are incorporated in this type of agreement.

In the majority of building conservation projects, based on standard conditions of contract, there will be references to the following two documents.

1. *Definition of Prime Cost of Daywork Carried Out Under a Building Contract* (Second edition, 1 December 1975). This is a publication issued under the joint names of the Royal Institution of Chartered Surveyors and the National Federation of Building Trades Employers (now the Building Employers' Confederation).
2. The RICS *Schedule of Basic Plant Charges For Use In Connection With Daywork Under a Building Contract* (Fourth revision, 1 January 1990).

The *Definition of Prime Cost of Daywork* contains six separate sections. These are:

Section 1 – Application
Section 2 – Composition of total charges
Section 3 – Labour
Section 4 – Materials and goods
Section 5 – Plant
Section 6 – Incidental costs, overheads and profit.

It is not proposed to repeat the content of the above 'definition' and all involved with works activities should purchase their own copies for reference purposes from either the RICS or the BEC.

When using the above 'definition' it will be found that there are references to other bodies who are involved in the agreement of standard wage rates, annual and public holiday agreements, guaranteed minimum weekly earnings, differentials or extra payments in respect of skill, responsibility, discomfort, inconvenience or risk, and other contributions or payments which have to be made in respect of workmen. For the majority of employees in the building industry these matters are detailed, at considerable length, in the *Working Rule Agreement* published on behalf of the National Joint Council for the Building Industry. Copies of the *Working Rule Agreement* may be readily purchased from the London or regional offices of the Building Employers'

Confederation. Other working rules which may apply could include the *National Working Rules of the Joint Industry Boards for Plumbing Mechanical Engineering Services*. Other specialist crafts such as those for electricians also have their own agreements which may need to be consulted for labour in daywork.

The publication previously referred to and entitled the RICS *Schedule of Basic Plant Charges For Use In Connection With Daywork Under a Building Contract* is obtainable from the RICS Bookshop or from the BCIS, 85–7 Clarence Street, Kingston-upon-Thames, Surrey KT1 1RB.

The daywork example which follows is meant to be incorporated in a lump sum contract incorporating bills of quantities. It is assumed that the quantity surveyor has decided to include the provision for daywork as a separate section at the end of Bill No. 1 and immediately following or in front of the separate section dealing with archaeological finds. Some quantity surveyors may prefer to include a daywork section in a separate bill dealing with all other provisional sums. Others may wish to carry the daywork total direct to the Main Summary. The precise location of the daywork provisions within a bill of quantities is really a matter of personal choice provided that it is kept in mind that whatever the allowances may be it is essentially a contingency allowance.

Many smaller building conservation contracts do not incorporate a bill of quantities but are based on drawings and specification only. The need for daywork provisions within such contracts is just as great as, or probably greater than, where bills of quantities are employed. It is a relatively easy matter to utilize the pricing document which follows by making it part of a tender package as issued to all tenderers and requiring the daywork allowances to be priced in detail and incorporated in a tender summary. If this practice is followed then a properly priced daywork schedule will be available for use during the running of the contract.

Job title:		Bill 1 – daywork (all provisional)	

Daywork (all provisional)

Item		£	p
	Notes		
A	This Bill Section is for Daywork executed in pursuance of Condition 13.5 of the Form of Contract hereinbefore referred to.		

Job title: Bill 1 – daywork
                                               (all provisional)

Item			£	p
B	The *DEFINITION OF PRIME COST OF DAYWORK CARRIED OUT UNDER A BUILDING CONTRACT* (Second edition, 1 December 1975) published by the RICS and the NFBTE (now BEC) applies subject to any amendments stated below.			
C	Authorized overtime on Daywork which has been worked on the written instructions of the Architect shall only be chargeable in the terms of prior written agreement between the parties to the building contract. In the absence of such prior agreement the Contractor will be reimbursed for the net additional cost calculated in accordance with the Working Rule Agreement and with an abatement of 50 per cent in respect of the percentage allowances for Incidental Costs, Overheads and Profit which is inserted by the tenderer in Item H on page 128 which follows.			
D	The Prime Cost of Plant referred to in Section 5 of the aforementioned 'Definition of Prime Cost' shall include, insofar as such items are chargeable to Prime Cost, those rates and allowances contained in the RICS *Schedule of Basic Plant Charges* (Fourth revision, 1 January 1990).			
E	The tenderer shall add to the Prime Cost of Daywork the amounts, if any, which he requires in respect of Incidental Costs, Overheads and Profit as defined at Section 6 of the abovementioned 'Definition of Prime Cost'.			

Job title:

Bill 1 – daywork
(all provisional)

Item		£	p
	Daywork (all provisional) (cont'd)		
F	Any reimbursement of VAT shall be by separate calculation made under Condition 15 of the Form of Contract hereinbefore referred to including the Supplemental Provisions (the VAT Agreement).		
	Labour		
G	Include the Provisional Sum of £____ for the Prime Cost of Labour in Daywork calculated in accordance with Section 3 of the aforementioned 'Definition of Prime Cost' and having regard to Item C on page 127.	*NB* Quantity Surveyor to insert an appropriate sum in here	
H	*Add* to last for Incidental Costs, Overheads and Profit as defined in Section 6.	%	
	Materials and goods		
I	Include the Provisional Sum of £____ for the Prime Cost of Materials and Goods calculated in accordance with Section 4 of the aforementioned 'Definition of Prime Cost'.	*NB* Quantity Surveyor to insert an appropriate sum in here	
J	*Add* to last for Incidental Costs, Overheads and Profit as defined in Section 6.	%	
	Plant		
K	Include the Provisional Sum of £____ for the Prime Cost of Plant calculated in accordance with Section 5 of the aforementioned 'Definition of Prime Cost' and having regard to Item D on page 127.	*NB* Quantity Surveyor to insert an appropriate sum in here	
L	*Add* to last for Incidental Costs, Overheads and Profit as defined in Section 6.	%	

Job title: Bill 1 — daywork
                                                            (all provisional)

COLLECTION   £   p

       From Page 126

       From   " 127

       From   " 128

       From   " 129

Daywork (all provisional)
Carried to Bill 1 Summary
   (or Main Summary)   £

Appendix C

Principal conditions of contract used in building conservation

Each of the principal Conditions of Contract are listed below and summarized in the pages which follow. Their application and a commentary listing the particular features, advantages and disadvantages are tabulated.

It is sound practice to decide upon the conditions to be used at an early stage in the design process; this is because the selection will influence the content and format of other documents such as the specification and bills of quantities.

In making a selection of contract type it is the responsibility of the design team to advise and guide the client in making a choice which best represents his overall interests.

Case law and practice continues to evolve. It is therefore necessary to ensure that project documentation always incorporates references to the full list of amendments and revisions which may be applicable to the conditions of contract as at the date of tender. All references to amendments and revisions which may be contained within this appendix must therefore be scrutinized and updated as necessary before being incorporated in project documentation.

CONDITIONS REFERRED TO

JCT   Standard Form of Building Contract 1980 edition; Private with quantities

JCT   Standard Form of Building Contract 1980 edition; Local authorities version with quantities

JCT   Standard Form of Building Contract 1980 edition; Private with approximate quantities

JCT   Standard Form of Building Contract 1980 edition; Local authorities version with approximate quantities

JCT Intermediate (IFC84) Form of Building Contract

JCT Standard Form of Building Contract 1980 edition; Private without quantities

JCT Standard Form of Building Contract 1980 edition; Local authorities version without quantities

JCT Agreement for Minor Building Works

JCT Standard Form of Measured Term Contract 1989 edition

JCT Standard Conditions of Contract for Building Work of a Jobbing Character; JA/C90

JCT Fixed Fee Form of Prime Cost Contract for Building Works

JCT Standard Form of Management Contract 1987 edition

JCT Standard Form of Building Contract with Contractor's Design 1981 edition

ACA Form of Building Agreement 1982, Second edition 1984

ACA Form of Building Agreement 1984, BPF Edition

ICE Conditions of Contract; Fifth edition (reprinted 1986)

ICE Conditions of Contract for Minor Works (1988)

General Conditions of Government Contracts for Building and Civil Engineering Works: Form GC/Works/1, Edition 2 – September 1977

General Conditions of Contract for Building and Civil Engineering Works: Form GC/Works/1, Edition 3 – December 1989

General Conditions of Government Contracts for Building and Civil Engineering Minor Works: Form GC/Works/2, Edition 2 – January 1980

General Conditions of Government Contracts for Building, Civil Engineering, Mechanical and Electrical Small Works: C1001, Second edition 1985

Daywork Term Contracts (reference only)

Form of contract	*Application*	*Comments*		
		Features	*Advantages*	*Disadvantages*
JCT Standard Form of Building Contract 1980 edition (Incorporating Amendments 1, 2, 4, 5 and 6) **Private with quantities** *Note* Amendment 7 needed for SMM7. Amendment 8 needed for revisions to VAT provisions. Amendment 9 needed for sundry revisions and to take account of a decision of the Court of Appeal.	Major lump sum building contracts in the private sector. Intended for where the work is substantially pre-planned. May be let on firm price basis (usually if contract does not exceed 2 years) or with fluctuation provisions (normally if contract exceeds 2 years).	Contains provisions for: 1. power to issue instructions; 2. interim payments and retention rules; 3. clerk of works (if wanted); 4. means of dealing with variations and provisional sums; 5. payment for unfixed materials; 6. defects liability period and making good; 7. partial possession (if wanted); 8. insurances against injury to persons or property; 9. insurance of the works (alternative clauses); 10. liquidated damages; 11. dates for possession and completion; 12. extensions of time; 13. powers of determination;	1. Well known; 2. compehensive; 3. includes bound in articles of agreement and separate Appendix for insertion of important matters.	1. Because of its drafting tends to be the subject of arbitration or litigation; 2. complicated and disliked nomination provisions; 3. specification not a contract document. Description of materials and workmanship to be in the bills. In conflict with CPI.

Form of contract	Application	Comments		
		Features	Advantages	Disadvantages
JCT Standard Form of Building Contract 1980 edition (Incorporating Amendments 1, 2, 4, 5 and 6) **Private with quantities** (cont'd) Amendment 10 needed for revised 1991 nomination procedure. May be supplemented by a 'Contractor's Designed Portion Supplement' where a contractor designs a portion of the works.		14. nominated sub-contractors and nominated suppliers; 15. antiquities (equivalent to an archaeological finds provision); 16. firm price or fluctuation provisions (optional clauses); 17. arbitration.		

Form of contract	Application	Comments		
		Features	Advantages	Disadvantages
JCT Standard Form of Building Contract 1980 edition (Incorporating Amendments 1, 2, 4, 5 and 6) **Local authorities version with quantities**	Major lump sum building contracts let by many local authorities. Intended for where the work is substantially pre-planned. May be let on firm price basis or with fluctuation provisions as stated for the 'Private With Quantities' version.	Essentially the same as for the 'Private With Quantities' edition but modified to meet the requirements of local authorities.	As stated for 'Private with quantities' edition.	As stated for 'Private with quantities' edition.
Note Refer to 'Private With Quantities' edition for listed additional Amendments and Supplement.				

Form of contract	Application	Comments		
		Features	Advantages	Disadvantages
JCT Standard Form of Building Contract 1980 edition (Incorporating Amendments 1, 2, 4, 5 and 6) **Private with approximate quantities** *Note:* Amendment 7 needed for SMM7. Amendment 8 needed for revisions to VAT provisions.	Major re-measurement building contracts in the Private Sector. Intended for where a project is not designed in sufficient detail to enable firm quantities to be prepared at tender stage. The quoted tender price, although a lump sum, is not a firm price. May be let on firm price basis or with fluctuation provisions	Contains provisions for: 1. measurement and valuation of the whole of the works and determination of a Final Sum in substitution of the tender price referred to in the contract bills; 2. power to issue instructions; 3. interim payments and retention rules; 4. clerk of works (if wanted); 5. means of dealing with variations and provisional sums; 6. payment for unfixed materials; 7. defects liability period and making good; 8. partial possession (if wanted); 9. insurances against injury to persons or property; 10. insurance of the works (alternative clauses); 11. liquidated damages;	1. Permits earlier start on site; 2. well known; 3. comprehensive; 4. Includes bound in articles of agreement and separate appendix for insertion of important matters.	1. Because of its drafting may be the subject of arbitration or litigation; 2. complicated and disliked nomination provisions; 3. specification not a contract document. Description of materials and workmanship to be in the bills. In conflict with CPI.

continued overleaf

Form of contract	Application	Comments		
		Features	Advantages	Disadvantages
JCT Standard Form of Building Contract 1980 edition (Incorporating Amendments 1, 2, 4, 5 and 6) **Private with approximate quantities** (cont'd) revisions and to take account of a decision of the Court of Appeal. Amendment 10 needed for revised 1991 nomination procedure.	depending on the contract period.	12. dates for possession and completion; 13. extensions of time; 14. powers of determination; 15. nominated sub-contractors and nominated suppliers; 16. antiquities (equivalent to an archaeological finds provision); 17. firm price or fluctuation provisions (optional clauses); 18. arbitration.		

Form of contract	Application	Comments		
		Features	Advantages	Disadvantages
JCT Standard Form of Building Contract 1980 edition (Incorporating Amendments 1, 2, 4, 5 and 6) **Local authorities version with approximate quantities**	Major re-measurement building contracts for local authorities. Intended for where a project is not designed in sufficient detail to enable firm quantities to be prepared at tender stage.	Essentially the same as for the 'Private with approximate quantities' edition but modified to meet the requirements of local authorities.	As stated for 'Private with approximate quantities' edition.	As stated for 'Private with approximate quantities' edition.
Note Refer to 'Private with approximate quantities' edition for listed additional Amendments.	The quoted tender price, although a lump sum, is not a firm price. May be let on firm price basis or with fluctuation provisions depending on the contract period.			

Form of contract	Application	Comments		
		Features	Advantages	Disadvantages
JCT Intermediate (IFC84) Form of Building Contract (Incorporating Amendments 1, 2 and 3) *Note* Amendment 4 needed if Bills incorporated on basis of SMM7. Amendment 5 needed for revisions to VAT provisions.	Building contracts of simple lump sum content up to about £300 000 estimated value. In practice IFC84 is used on larger projects because of the problems encountered with the nomination provisions of the JCT Standard Form of Building Contract 1980 edition. Originally intended to be used for contracts of not exceeding 12 months but is often used on contracts of up to (cont'd)	Contains provisions for: 1. drawings to be supplemented by Specification and/ or Schedules of Work (optional). Bills are also optional but should be used on complex and higher value projects (say if in excess of £150 000); 2. power to issue instructions by architect/contract administrator 3. interim payments and retention rules; 4. clerk of works (if wanted); 5. means of dealing with variations and provisional sums; 6. payment for unfixed materials; 7. defects liability period and making good; 8. insurances against injury to persons or property; 9. insurance of the works (alternative clauses); 10. liquidated damages;	1. Becoming increasingly well known. 2. reasonably comprehensive. Much more versatile if bills incorporated; 3. includes bound in agreement and separate appendix for insertion of important matters.	1. Not suitable if complex services installations or other highly specialized work involved. 2. no nomination procedure for PC sums; 3. no specific provision for sectional completion; 4. no clause dealing specifically with antiquities or archaeological finds.

Form of contract	Application	Comments		
		Features	*Advantages*	*Disadvantages*
JCT Intermediate (IFC84) Form of Building Contract (Incorporating Amendments 1, 2, and 3) (cont'd)	2 years when full fluctuation provisions are not required.	11. dates for possession and completion; 12. extensions of time; 13. powers of determination; 14. naming of persons to act as sub-contractors (priced by contractor in tender); 15. arbitration.		

Form of contract	Application	Comments		
		Features	Advantages	Disadvantages
JCT Standard Form of Building Contract 1980 edition (Incorporating Amendments 1, 2, 3, 4, 5 and 6) **Private without quantities** *Note* Amendment 8 needed for revisions to VAT provisions. Amendment 9 needed for sundry revisions and to take account of a decision of the Court of Appeal. Amendment 10 needed for revised 1991 nomination procedure.	Best suited for lump sum building contracts of not exceeding about £150 000 estimated value in the private sector.	Contains provisions for: 1. the specification to be a contract document; 2. a schedule of work to be provided for pricing by the contractor (optional); 3. the employer to call for the contractor to provide: a) a Contract sum analysis (optional); b) a Schedule of Rates on which the Contract Sum is based (optional); 4. power to issue instructions; 5. interim payments and retention rules; 6. clerk of works (if wanted); 7. means of dealing with variations and provisional sums; 8. payments for unfixed materials; 9. defects liability period and making good;	1. Well known; 2. comprehensive provided significant variations are not anticipated; 3. includes bound in articles of agreement and separate appendix for insertion of important matters.	1. Because of its drafting tends to be the subject of arbitration or litigation; 2. complicated and disliked nomination provisions; 3. absence of a bill may make the agreement of variations difficult.

Form of contract	Application	Comments		
		Features	Advantages	Disadvantages
JCT Standard Form of Building Contract 1980 edition (Incorporating Amendments 1, 2, 3, 4, 5 and 6) **Private with quantities** (cont'd)		10. partial possession (if wanted); 11. insurances against injury to persons or property; 12. insurance of the works (alternative clauses); 13. liquidated damages; 14. dates for possession and completion; 15. extensions of time; 16. powers of determination; 17. nominated sub-contractors and nominated suppliers; 18. antiquities (equivalent to an archaeological finds provision); 19. firm price or fluctuation provisions (optional clauses); 20. arbitration.		

Form of contract	Application	Comments		
		Features	Advantages	Disadvantages
JCT Standard Form of Building Contract 1980 edition (Incorporating Amendments 1, 2, 3, 4, 5 and 6) **Local authorities version without quantities**	Best suited for lump sum building contracts of not exceeding about £150 000 estimated value let by many local authorities.	Essentially the same as for the 'Private without quantities' edition but modified to meet the requirements of local authorities.	As stated for 'Private without quantities' edition.	As stated for 'Private without quantities' edition.
Note Refer to 'Private without quantities' edition for listed additional amendments.				

Form of contract	Application	Comments		
		Features	Advantages	Disadvantages
JCT Agreement for Minor Building Works (Incorporating all Revisions up to September 1989 and including the bound in Supplementary Memorandum MWS 1989) *Note* Part E of Supplementary Memorandum MWS 1989 in respect of the BEC Guarantee Scheme may be incorporated or omitted.	Minor lump sum building works of a simple content of up to about £100 000 estimated value. Intended for projects of short duration (say not exceeding 1 year) when full fluctuation provisions are not required.	Contains provisions for: 1. use of drawings and/or specification and/or schedules; 2. right to issue clarifications and instructions; 3. progress payments and retention rules (optional); 4. means of dealing with variations and provisional sums (optional); 5. payment for unfixed materials; 6. defects liability period and making good (optional); 7. liablity for injury to persons and property; 8. insurance of the works (alternative clauses); 9. liquidated damages (optional); 10. dates for commencement and completion; 11. extensions of time; 12. powers of determination;	1. simple and easy to follow. 2. includes bound in agreement.	1. No provision for nominations; 2. no specific provision for clerk of works; 3. no clause dealing specifically with antiquities or archaeological finds; 4. no provisions for dealing with contractual claims.

Form of contract	Application	Comments		
		Features	Advantages	Disadvantages
JCT Standard Form of Measured Term Contract 1989 edition *Note* Refer to Practice Note MTC/1 and Guide. This also includes a sample Order Form.	Intended for use by the larger clients or local authorities who have an estate to maintain, where there is a continuity of maintenance and minor works including improvements, and where the estimated annual value of expenditure is likely to exceed say £100 000. The contract is activated by the issue, from time to time, of a series of separate orders defining the work required.	Contains provisions for: 1. work to be measured as actually performed and generally priced on basis of pre-priced schedules of rates; 2. prices in schedule of rates to be updated on a yearly or other basis or alternatively prices may be fixed (the latter is unsuitable to MTCs in excess of 2 years); 3. the contract period (the 'term') is usually for a stipulated period of not less than 1 year (preferably longer and 3 years is here suggested); 4. properties to be listed where work is likely; 5. employer to decide on type of work required; 6. minimum and maximum Order values; 7. assessment of anticipated value of work required per annum to be stated; no guarantee;	1. Extremely flexible for day-to-day maintenance and related work; 2. although only recently introduced has the benefit of close similarity with the long-standing PSA MTC Conditions; 3. includes bound in Articles of agreement and separate appendix.	1. Requires a relatively high level of supervision and monitoring; 2. depending on the schedule selected may not include sufficient rates for work to ancient monuments and historic buildings.

Form of contract	Application	Comments		
		Features	Advantages	Disadvantages
JCT Standard Form of Measured Term Contract 1989 edition (cont'd)	Not intended to apply to mechanical and electrical services.	8. definition of schedule of rates to be used (e.g. PSA Schedule or the National Schedule of rates); 9. preliminaries and specification requirements must be included in the schedule of rates; 10. tenderers invited to quote percentage addition/ deduction applicable to the pre-printed schedule of rates; 11. daywork; 12. orders to be measured and valued by the contracts administrator or contractor (optional); 13. progress payments; 14. making good defects; 15. insurances against injury to persons or property; 16. insurance of existing structures; 17. all risks insurance; 18. determination; 19. break clause permitting either party to end the contract; 20. arbitration.		

Form of contract	Application	Comments		
		Features	Advantages	Disadvantages
JCT Standard Conditions of Contract for Building Works of a Jobbing Character; JA/C90	Lump sum jobbing work. Intended for local authorities and others in the private sector for contracts of up to about £10000 and of short duration. May be used in conjunction with the standard tender and agreement (JA/T90) or by employers who wish to place jobbing contracts by means of their own works orders.	Contains provisions for: 1. description of works or issue of drawings with or without a specification; 2. employer's power to issue instructions including variations; 3. payments on account may be introduced if contract period exceeds 1 month; 4. defects liability period; 5. payment dependent on contractor's issue of an invoice; 6. insurance against injury to persons or property; 7. insurance (by employer) of existing structure, works and unfixed materials against fire and other risks; 8. dates for commencement and completion; 9. arbitration.	1. Simple and clear; 2. covers most essential provisions; 3. standard form of tender and agreement available (JA/T90) (optional).	1. Few if limited to simple low value work without variations; 2. no provision for the appointment of an architect or contract administrator; 3. no specific provision for work by nominated sub-contractors; 4. no clause dealing specifically with antiquities or archaeological finds.

Form of contract	Application	Comments		
		Features	Advantages	Disadvantages
JCT Fixed Fee Form of Prime Cost Contract for Building works (October 1976 Revision incorporating Amendments F4/1976 and F5/1987)	For 'cost plus' activities. Intended for building Works when decision taken to dispense with lump sum or re-measurement methods of contracting and when an MTC is considered inappropriate. Most suited for emergency work and operations of a similar nature or where pre-	Contains provisions for: 1. contractor to be reimbursed all his costs (the 'prime cost') plus an agreed fixed fee; 2. requires a pre-estimate to be determined before a meaningful 'fixed fee' can be inserted by tenderers; 3. contract to be implemented without drawings; 4. power to issue instructions but not to vary the nature or scope of the works; 5. interim payments and retention rules; 6. clerk of works (if wanted); 7. payment for unfixed materials; 8. defects liability period and making good; 9. partial possession if contractor consents; 10. insurances against injury to persons or property;	1. Prompt start on site; 2. comprehensive; 3. Includes bound in agreement, definition of prime cost, provision for the insertion of the fixed fee, an appendix and a supplemental agreement.	1. No initial contract sum; 2. difficult to accurately assess the pre-estimate which is required; 3. quality of assembly of 'prime cost' details often variable. Time consuming work in checking their validity;

continued overleaf

Form of contract	Application	Comments		
		Features	Advantages	Disadvantages
JCT Fixed Fee Form of Prime Cost Contract for Building works (October 1976 Revision incorporating Amendments F4/1976 and F5/1987) (cont'd)	planning is being dispensed with. Client must accept lower than normal standards of financial control. No financial limits on value of work to be performed.	11. insurance of the works (alternative clauses); 12. liquidated damages; 13. dates for possession and completion; 14. extensions of time; 15. powers of determination; 16. nominated sub-contractors and nominated suppliers; 17. direct contracts (optional); 18. antiquities (equivalent to archaeological finds provision); 19. arbitration.		4. difficult to avoid payment for rectifying mistakes which occur during the progress of the works; 5. poor financial control; 6. Risk that cost of works may exceed a client's original expectations.

Form of contract	Application	Comments		
		Features	*Advantages*	*Disadvantages*
JCT Standard Form of Management Contract 1987 edition *Note* Amendment 1 needed for amendments to Section 9 'Settlement of disputes – Arbitration'. See 'Phased Completion Supplement' where project is to be completed in Phases.	A non-lump sum management contract where the employer requires a building contractor (the management contractor) to plan, coordinate, organize, supervise and generally manage and secure the construction and completion of the entire project but where the	Contains provisions for: 1. Appointment of the employer's own professional team (usually architect, quantity surveyor and possibly engineers). 2. this not being a lump sum contract the quantity surveyor is required to prepare a Cost Plan (indication of the total cost) which is subject to the consent of the management contractor; 3. the actual costs incurred by the management contractor (referred to as the 'Prime Cost') is amount actually payable by employer plus the agreed management fee (either lump sum or percentage); 4. the management contractor to be reimbursed his own on-site management and on-site services and facilities as part of the 'Prime Cost'.	1. Can produce good results given full co-operation and liaison between the employer, his/her own design team and the management contractor; 2. earlier starts and earlier completions may be possible (subject to 1. above);	1. Complex contractual relationships; 2. probably more expensive than traditional methods of procurement; 3. final cost cannot be forecast with confidence until the whole of the works is well advanced; 4. only suitable for very large

continued overleaf

Form of contract	Application	Comments		
		Features	Advantages	Disadvantages
JCT Standard Form of Management Contract 1987 edition (cont'd) Refer to Practice Note MC/1 for general guidance. *Note* Because of the complex nature of this form of contract it is necessary to refer to the management contract conditions proper. This commentary is intended to cover references to particular features only.	employer wishes to retain his own independent design team. The management contractor does not normally undertake any construction work but provides common on-site facilities. This contract should only be used if employer wishes to: 1. retain an independent design team; 2. wishes to achieve early completion;	5. detailed drawings, specification and Bills prepared (by professional teams) at appropriate times for all the separate Works contracts; 6. management contractor enters into individual works contracts so as to ensure completion of the whole; 7. employer and Management Contractor to enter into an agreement containing two phases: (a) Pre-construction period; (b) construction period; 8. pre-construction period management fee to become due for the duties stated;	3. probably some 80% of the prime cost will be tendered for in competition; 4. includes bound in articles of agreement, conditions of contract divided into 9 Sections covering both specific and customary obligations and liabilities of the parties, schedules dealing with 'description of the project', definition of 'prime cost' and 'services to be provided by the	schemes of conservation; 5. quality control is more difficult.

Form of contract	Application	Comments		
		Features	Advantages	Disadvantages
JCT Standard Form of Management Contract 1987 edition (cont'd)	3. obtain good competition for each of the separate works contracts; 4. Accept the risk/probability that the cost may be higher than with a traditional procurement method.	9. employer to decide whether to instruct management contractor to proceed to commence and complete construction or whether not to proceed; 10. construction period duties of management contractor to be defined. 11. payment to be made to management contractor for various works contracts plus instalments of the management fee as the work proceeds.	management contractor', 'list of drawings', and a 'list of site facilities' to be provided by the management contractor.	

Form of contract	Application	Comments		
		Features	*Advantages*	*Disadvantages*
JCT Standard Form of Building Contract With Contractor's Design 1981 edition incorporating Amendments 1, 2, 3 and 4 *Note* Amendment 5 needed for revisions to the VAT provisions. Amendment 6 needed for sundry revisions and to take account of a decision of the Court of Appeal.	A lump sum contract intended for use when a contractor is responsible for design as well as for construction. Customary for the employer to prepare, with professional assistance, a detailed performance specification. The contract does not provide for an employer's architect or quantity surveyor to be named in	Contains provisions for: 1. the contractor to be liable for design, selection of materials and provision of workmanship to satisfy the previously stated requirements of the employer; 2. important contract documents include: (a) the employer's requirements; (b) the contractor's proposals; (c) the contract sum analysis; 3. a lump sum price (with provision for stage or periodic payments) but subject to adjustments as described; 4. appointment of the employer's agent who shall have access to the works (including off-site locations); 5. power of employer to issue instruction; 6. materials, goods and workmanship generally to be as stated in the 'employer's requirements' or in the 'contractor's proposals';	1. Earlier starts and earlier completion should be possible; 2. places entire responsibility on contractor; 3. includes bound in articles of agreement, supplementary provisions and appendices for insertion of important matters.	1. Usually more expensive than traditional methods of procurement; 2. supervision and monitoring difficult; 3. quality of work can suffer; 4. lack of definition in either the 'employer's requirements' or in the 'contractor's proposals' can lead to disputes and extra cost; 5. only suitable for very large schemes of conservation.

Form of contract	Application	Comments		
		Features	*Advantages*	*Disadvantages*
JCT Standard Form of Building Contract with Contractor's Design 1981 edition Incorporating Amendments 1, 2, 3 and 4 (cont'd) Refer also to Practice Note CD/1B.	the contract but there is provision for an 'employer's agent'. Customary for the employer to require the contractor to submit proposals prior to entering into a contract.	7. interim payments and retention rules; 8. valuation rules for dealing with variations; 9. defects liability period and making good; 10. partial possession subject to contractor's consent; 11. insurances against injury to persons or property; 12. insurance of the works (alternative clauses); 13. liquidated damages;	14. dates for possession and completion; 15. extensions of time; 16. powers of determination; 17. employer may stipulate 'named' sub-contractors; 18. antiquities (equivalent to an archaeological finds provisions); 19. substantially firm price or fluctuations (options); 20. contractor's design warranty and limit of contractor's design liability; 21. arbitration.	

Form of contract	Application	Comments		
		Features	*Advantages*	*Disadvantages*
ACA Form of Building Agreement 1982, Second edition 1984 *Note* Refer to the *Guide to the ACA Form of Building Agreement* (Second edition). This Agreement also referred to as 'ACA2'.	A lump sum building contract for use in the private/local authority sectors. Capable of considerable flexibility permitting either the architect responsible for design and the contractor responsible for construction or, as an alternative, the contractor may be made responsible for both design and construction.	Contains provisions for: 1. contract to include drawings and optional schedule of rates/ prices, optional specification and optional bills of quantities – if bills provided then schedule of rates becomes superseded; 2. appointment of either an architect or SO; 3. appointment of quantity surveyor (optional); 4. contractor may be required to submit drawings for approval (optional); 5. contractor responsible for supervision and management; 6. power to issue instructions; 7. interim payments and retention rules; 8. means of dealing with variations by contractor submitting estimates but with other means of valuation.	1. Optional design responsibility on contractor; 2. the several alternative clauses permit flexibility; 3. includes bound in agreement, time schedule and record of issue of information.	1. Not widely used; 2. little track record on conservation work compared to the JCT and governmental conditions.

Form of contract	Application	Comments		
		Features	Advantages	Disadvantages
ACA Form of Building Agreement 1982, Second edition 1984 (cont'd)		9. maintenance period and making good;		
		10. sectional completion (optional);		
		11. insurances against personal injury and liability for properties;		
		12. insurance of the works (alternative clauses);		
		13. liquidated damages;		
		14. dates for possession and completion;		
		15. extensions of time;		
		16. acceleration or postponement clause;		
		17. powers of termination;		
		18. named sub-contractors and suppliers;		
		19. antiquities (equivalent to an archaeological finds provision);		
		20. firm price or fluctuation provisions (optional);		
		21. adjudication and/or arbitration.		

Form of contract	Application	Comments		
		Features	Advantages	Disadvantages
ACA Form of Building Agreement 1984, BPF edition	This is an adaptation of the ACA Form of Building Agreement to suit the specific requirements of the British Property Federation (BPF) and with a greater contractor involvement. The principal differences in this BPF Edition are referred to in the comments.	The main provisions are very similar to those in the ACA Form of Building Agreement 1982 (Second edition, 1984) but: • use of client's representative (not specifically an architect); • a schedule of activities is offered as an option to Bills; • the contractor is required to supplement drawings or other information provided by the client's representatives; • the contractor is responsible for all errors in documentation provided by him; • those parts of the works designed by the contractor are to be 'fit for purpose'; • the client's representative has authority to issue instructions; • reference to provisional sums (clauses 9.4 and 9.5) are omitted.	1. Greater design responsibility on contractor (also listed as a possible 'disadvantage'); 2. meets demands for 'buildability' to be considered at design stage; 3. earlier starts and earlier completions may be possible; 4. includes bound in agreement, time schedule and record of issue of information.	1. Greater design responsibility on contractor (also listed as a possible 'advantage'); 2. use mainly limited to major private clients; 3. little track record on conservation work compared to the JCT and governmental conditions.

Form of contract	Application	Comments		
		Features	Advantages	Disadvantages
ICE Conditions of Contract: Fifth edition (re-printed 1986) *Note* A sixth edition of the ICE Conditions of Contract is in the course of preparation. When available appropriate notes may be inserted on page 173.	Major re-measurement works of a civil engineering nature. Should only be considered for conservation work which is of a heavy engineering nature and where an engineer is engaged to look after the employer's interests. Examples of suitable conservation work	Contains provisions for: 1. the 'contract' to include the conditions of contract, specification, drawings, priced bills of quantities, the tender and written acceptance thereof and the contract agreement (if completed); 2. the quantities set out in the bills are estimated only and are not to be taken as the actual or correct quantities; 3. the 'contract price' is only known after complete re-measurement when it supersedes the 'tender total'; 4. the 'engineer' has extremely wide powers; 5. power to issue instructions; 6. performance bond if wanted (optional); 7. monthly payments and retention rules; 8. right of interest on over-due payments;	1. Well known; 2. compre-hensive; 3. great responsibility is placed on the contractor and this is clearly stated; 4. permits a contractor to use his ingenuity over temporary works; 5. includes bound in form of tender, appendix, form of agreement and form of bond.	1. Difficulty for clients in not knowing their likely total financial commitment at the commencement of the contract; 2. not best suited for associated building work involving complex or detailed pre-planning of the design.

continued overleaf

Form of contract	Application	Comments		
		Features	Advantages	Disadvantages
ICE Conditions of Contract: Fifth edition (re-printed 1986) (cont'd)	include stone viaducts, sea defences, bridges, piers, etc. The 'tender total' is the total of the priced bills of quantities at the date of acceptance and should not be regarded as a firm price. It is an indicative cost only.	9. engineer's representative (or clerk of works); 10. payment for unfixed materials; 11. period of maintenance and consequential repairs; 12. sectional completion (if wanted); 13. indemnity against injury to persons or property; 14. insurance of the works, etc.; 15. liquidated damages; 16. dates for possession and time for completion; 17. nominated sub-contractors; 18. provisional sums/prime cost sums; 19. facility to incorporate special conditions (e.g. contract price fluctuations); 20. arbitration.		

Form of contract	Application	Comments		
		Features	Advantages	Disadvantages
ICE Conditions of Contract for Minor Works: First edition (January 1988)	Minor Civil Engineering Works, usually of a lump sum or remeasurement nature, where: 1. work is simple, straight-forward and generally fully pre-planned; 2. estimated contract value is low (say not exceeding £100 000); 3. period for completion does not exceed 6 months (subject to proviso).	Contains provisions for: 1. the 'Contract' to include the Conditions of Contract, the appendix thereto, drawings and specification, together with those documents which have not been deleted at 2 below; 2. the deletion of references to whichever of the following are inapplicable: • bills of quantities; • schedules of rates; • daywork schedules; 3. the appendix to state that the contract will incorporate whichever of the following are appropriate: • lump sum; • measure and value using bills of quantities; • valuation based on a schedule of rates; • valuation based on daywork; • cost plus fee.	1. Sufficiently comprehensive and flexible for most low value civil engineering projects; 2. best when lump sum tenders invited; 3. includes bound in agreement, the contract schedule (list of documents forming part of the contract) and an appendix.	1. Final Cost and tender price can vary significantly in absence of lump sum tender requirements; 2. no specific nomination clauses; 3. few other disadvantages if used in the way intended and for simple projects.

continued overleaf

Form of contract	Application	Comments		
		Features	Advantages	Disadvantages
ICE Conditions of Contract for Minor Works: First edition (January 1988) (cont'd)		4. engineer's powers to give instructions, including variations; 5. interim payments and retention rules; 6. payment for unfixed materials; 7. right of interest on overdue payments; 8. defects correction period and making good; 9. insurances against damage to persons and property; 10. insurance of the works (optional); 11. liquidated damages; 12. starting date and period for completion; 13. sectional completion (if wanted); 14. contractor not responsible for design of permanent work (except as noted); 15. contractor to submit final account for engineer's approval or otherwise; 16. conciliation or arbitration.		

Form of contract	Application	Comments		
		Features	*Advantages*	*Disadvantages*
General Conditions of Government Contracts for Building and Civil Engineering Works: Form GC/Works/1, Edition 2 – September 1977 *Note* When used by non-government departments (e.g. as by English Heritage and others) requires the introduction of supplementary conditions.	Major lump sum or re-measurement type building or civil engineering contracts principally in the public sector. Commonly used when estimated value is likely to exceed about £150 000 and with no upper limit. Also used on complex projects of smaller value. May be let on firm price basis (usually if contract does not exceed 2 years) or with	Contains provisions for: 1. contract to include drawings, specification and usually bills of quantities or schedules of rates; 2. design team left with choice of: • firm bills of quantities, or • provisional bills of quantities, or • approximate bills of quantities, or • schedule of rates; 3. separate abstract of particulars to be provided covering such matters as those referred to at 10, 15, 16 and 21 below; 4. wide powers to issue instructions; 5. role of SO may be exercised by any building or engineering professional acting for the authority; 6. interim payments and reserve (retention) rules; 7. clerk of works or resident engineer (if wanted);	1. Well known; 2. very clear except for insurance provision; 3. comprehensive; 4. specification is a contract document – complies with CPI; 5. nomination arrangements well liked by clients; 6. claims are relatively infrequent; 7. readily amended to suit	1. Need for separate abstract of particulars; 2. need for incorporation of supplementary conditions; 3. some insurances which are the responsibility of the contractor appear only in the bills of quantities (preliminaries). Nevertheless the contractor is fully at risk unless an 'accepted risk' applies.

continued overleaf

Form of contract	Application	Comments		
		Features	Advantages	Disadvantages
General Conditions of Government Contracts for Building and Civil Engineering Works: Form GC/Works/1, Edition 2 – September 1977 (cont'd)	variation of price fluctuation provisions (normally if contract exceeds 2 years).	8. means of dealing with variations, provisional sums, provisional quantities and PC sums; 9. payment for unfixed materials; 10. defects liability period and making good; 11. sectional completion (if wanted); 12. liability for injury to persons or property; 13. responsibility for the works and other things; 14. accepted risks; 15. liquidated damages; 16. date for completion from either the date of possession of site or order to commence; 17. extensions of time; 18. powers of determination; 19. nominated sub-contractors and nominated suppliers; 20. antiquities (archaeological finds provision); 21. firm price or with variation of price fluctuation provisions (optional); 22. arbitration.	private or public sector non-governmental clients.	

Form of contract	Application	Comments		
		Features	Advantages	Disadvantages
General Conditions of Contract for Building and Civil Engineering: GC/Works/1, Edition 3 – December 1989. Standard Form of Contract – Lump Sum With Quantities *Note* When used by non-government departments continued overleaf	Major lump sum building or civil engineering contracts principally in the public sector. Not suited in its present form for conservation work or works involving extensive alterations or repairs. This is a new innovative form of contract which,	This Edition 3 should be regarded as a completely new set of conditions of contract in its own right. The changes from Edition 2 of GC/Works/1 are so fundamental that it is wrong to regard Edition 3 as merely being an updated version of Edition 2.	It is premature to list these at the present stage.	See reference elsewhere to the present unsuitability for conservation work or works involving extensive alterations or repairs. These objections are likely to be overcome in subsequent versions of Edition 3.

continued overleaf

Form of contract	Application	Comments		
		Features	Advantages	Disadvantages
General Conditions of Contract for Building and Civil Engineering: GC/Works/1, Edition 3 – December 1989. Standard Form of Contract – Lump Sum With Quantities (cont'd) requires the introduction of supplementary conditions.	when developed to embrace contracts of a re-measurement type or those which are based only on drawings and specification, should prove to be the most comprehensive and clear range of conditions of contract available for the construction industry. Supplementary conditions may be introduced to make Edition 3 suitable for conservation and similar work.	Because Edition 3 has only been used to a limited extent since 1990, is likely to be subject to amendment, and is not considered suitable (in its present form) for building conservation work. It is inappropriate to make further commentary at this stage on what is effectively a new and developing set of conditions of contract.		

Form of contract	Application	Comments		
		Features	Advantages	Disadvantages
General Conditions of Government Contracts for Building and Civil Engineering Minor Works: Form GC/Works/ 2, Edition 2 – January 1980 *Note* When used by non-government departments (e.g. as by English Heritage and others) requires the introduction of supplementary conditions.	Lump sum building or civil engineering contracts principally in the public sector. Commonly used when estimated value is likely to range between about £15 000 and £150 000 and variations are possible. Applicable to firm price tenders. Should not be used when bills of quantities are required (use GC/Works/1 instead).	Contains provisions for: 1. contract to include drawings and a specification; 2. design team may elect to incorporate a summary of tender, a summary of PC and provisional sums, and a schedule of rates; 3. power to issue instructions; 4. role of SO may be exercised by any building or engineering person so designated by the authority; 5. interim payments and reserve (retention) rules; 6. means of dealing with variations, provisional sums and PC sums; 7. payment for unfixed materials; 8. defects liability period and making good; 9. liability for injury to persons or property;	1. Well known; 2. very clear except for insurance needs; 3. comprehensive apart from no provision for bills of quantities; 4. nomination arrangements well liked by clients; 5. claims are infrequent; 6. readily amended to suit private or public sector non-governmental clients.	1. Need for separate abstract of particulars; 2. need for incorporation of supplementary conditions; 3. need for contractor's insurances not described. Nevertheless the contractor is fully at risk unless an 'accepted risk' applies; 4. no specific provision for dealing with antiquities or archaeological finds but often

continued overleaf

Form of contract	*Application*	Comments		
		Features	*Advantages*	*Disadvantages*
General Conditions of Government Contracts for Building and Civil Engineering Minor Works: Form GC/Works/ 2, Edition 2 – January 1980 (cont'd)		10. responsibility for the works and other things; 11. accepted risks; 12. date for completion from either the date of possession of the site or order to commence; 13. extensions of time; 14. powers of determination; 15. nominated sub-contractors and nominated suppliers; 16. arbitration; 17. design team may elect to incorporate, by way of non-standard supplementary conditions, provisions for additional matters such as sectional completion, liquidated damages, daywork rates and archaeological finds.		written into contracts; 5. no provision for dealing with contractual claims.

Form of contract	Application	Comments		
		Features	Advantages	Disadvantages
General Conditions of Government Contracts for Building, Civil Engineering, Mechanical and Electrical Small Works: Form C1001, Second edition 1985 *Note* When used by non-government departments (e.g. as by English Heritage and others) requires the introduction of supplementary conditions.	Small lump sum building, civil engineering or mechanical and electrical contracts principally in the public sector. Intended for small works of a simple content of up to about £15 000 estimated value. Applicable to projects which are fully pre-planned, when variations are unlikely, and when firm price tenders are required.	Contains provisions for: 1. contract to include drawings and/or specification and/or schedules; 2. power to issue instructions (variations are not anticipated but may arise in practice); 3. role of SO may be exercised by any building or engineering person so designated by the authority; 4. progress payments may be allowed if the list of contract documents says so; 5. maintenance period and making good (only applicable if the list of contract documents says so); 6. liability for personal injury and loss of property; 7. responsibility for the works and other things; 8. payment dependent on contractor's issue of an invoice; 9. accepted risks; 10. commencement and date for completion to be as stated in the contract; 11. powers of termination by authority only.	1. Widely used by governmental organizations; 2. simple and very clear; 3. a glossary of terms is incorporated in the conditions; 4. readily amended to suit private or public sector non-governmental clients.	1. Few if limited to simple low value work without variations; 2. need for incorporation of simple supplementary conditions for non-governmental departments; 3. no provision for nomination; 4. no clause dealing specifically with antiquities or archaeological finds.

Form of contract	Application	Comments		
		Features	Advantages	Disadvantages
Daywork Term Contracts Currently there are no JCT conditions applicable to this type of work. Within the government estate the General Conditions for a Daywork Term Contract – form C1401 apply but these conditions are not presently available from HMSO.	There is the need in the non-governmental sector for a specially drafted set of contract conditions to be prepared dealing specifically with day-to-day jobbing work where the nature of the work does not lend itself to measurement (for which an MTC might be	The contract/agreement should make provision for: 1. naming the parties; 2. naming the site or sites; 3. a definition of the scope of the Contract; 4. describing direct contracts which may be carried out by others; 5. the estimated annual value or anticipated labour resources to be provided; 6. naming of SO and quantity surveyor; 7. contractor's general obligations and responsibilities; 8. power of SO to issue instructions and method of placing orders for the work;	Specially drafted sets of conditions for daywork term contracts could be made to fit the precise requirements of a client.	The time and fees involved in preparing such one-off sets of documentation for daywork term contracts. However, it is anticipated that, in practice, the documentation could be prepared quickly and with only a modest fee commitment.

Form of contract	Application	Comments			
		Features		Advantages	Disadvantages
Daywork Term Contracts (cont'd)	appropriate) but when there is a continuity of jobbing activities – perhaps spread over a number of buildings or over a large estate or involving a group of separate sites. It is not always possible to set up a system using a series of individual lump sum jobbing orders perhaps based on JCT JA/C90. The JCT Fixed Fee Form of Prime Cost Contract may also be inappropriate	9. issue of drawings and specifications; 10. statutory notices and obligations and estate regulations; 11. setting out, marking up, ordering of requirements, etc.; 12. labour, materials and workmanship; 13. supervision by contractor; 14. access by SO to all places of work; 15. clerk of works (if wanted);	16. defects liability and making good; 17. assignment and sub-letting; 18. use of the site/s; 19. responsibility for the existing premises; 20. overtime working; 21. safety, health and welfare; 22. injury to persons and property; 23. insurance of the works against fire and other risks; 24. accepted risks;		

continued overleaf

Form of contract	Application	Features	Comments	Advantages	Disadvantages
Daywork Term Contracts (cont'd)	because of the inability to place a sufficiently accurate assessment on the prime cost of the works. When the need for the application of a daywork term contract has been established then it is recommended that a purpose made set of documentation be prepared by a quantity surveyor well experienced in conservation work.	25. possession and completion for each order; 26. powers of determination; 27. nominated sub-contractors and nominated suppliers; 28. interim payments, retention and final payments for each order; 29. VAT; 30. arbitration; 31. schedule giving full definition of: • prime cost of labour; • prime cost of materials and goods; • prime cost of plant, consumable stores and	services; • prime cost of work sub-contracted or otherwise sub-let; 32. contract period and break clauses; 33. obligations on contractor to provide full documentation for all costs incurred including time sheets, wages books, invoices, delivery tickets and receipts; 34. tender form enabling tenderers to quote their percentage additions on the various elements of prime cost described at 31 above.		

Form of contract	Application	Comments		
		Features	Advantages	Disadvantages
Daywork Term Contracts (cont'd)	The JCT Fixed Fee Form of Prime Cost Contract could be redrafted by permitting tenderers to quote percentage additions on the different elements of cost which constitute the prime cost instead of quoting a single lump sum fixed fee. An alternative method of establishing a daywork term contract would be to prepare Conditions incorporating the RICS/BEC *Definition of Prime Cost of Daywork Carried Out Under a Building Contract*			

continued overleaf

Form of contract	Application	Comments		
		Features	Advantages	Disadvantages
Daywork Term Contracts (cont'd)	(Second edition, December 1975) together with the RICS *Schedule of Basic Plant Charges* (Fourth revision, January 1990). There are other methods of dealing with this deficiency in the range of available documentation but in all instances appropriate professional advice is essential. Whichever method is adopted it would be appropriate to include the matters referred to in the adjoining column headed 'Features' (see pages 168–70).			

NEW CONDITIONS OR AMENDMENTS

Note: This tabulated page is provided to enable the reader to insert brief particulars of any new Conditions of Contract or Amendments to existing Conditions of Contract which may be issued and which are relevant to building conservation

Form of contract	Application	Comments		
		Features	*Advantages*	*Disadvantages*

NEW CONDITIONS OR AMENDMENTS

Note: This tabulated page is provided to enable the reader to insert brief particulars of any new Conditions of Contract or Amendments to existing Conditions of Contract which may be issued and which are relevant to building conservation

Form of contract	*Application*	*Comments*		
		Features	*Advantages*	*Disadvantages*

Questionnaire for completion by general contractors

Chapter 13 deals with the occasions when a structured questionnaire needs to be issued to potential tenderers. This appendix may be used as the basis for issue to general contractors involved in conservation activities.

CONFIDENTIAL   File ref. _____

> QUESTIONNAIRE FOR GENERAL CONTRACTORS WISHING TO BE CONSIDERED FOR TENDERING ON CONSERVATION WORKS COMMISSIONED BY (NAME OF ORGANIZATION)

1. Name of company   . . . .

2. Registered office   . . . .

                              . . . .

                              . . . .

                              Tel. no. . . . .

                              Fax no. . . . .

3. Local office   . . . .

                              . . . .

                              . . . .

                              Tel. no. . . . .

                              Fax no. . . . .

4. Nature of company and date
   established   . . . .

5. Status of company (e.g. family business, partnership, sole proprietor) . . . .

6. Annual turnover (approx.) £ . . . .

7. Name of parent or holding company (if applicable) . . . .

8. Is company registered for VAT? (If yes, give registration no.) . . . .

9. Give brief details of any third party insurance (e.g. name of insurer and amount of cover)
. . . .
. . . .

10. Geographical area in which work normally carried out (state radius from office) . . . .

11. (a) How many craftsmen are permanently and directly employed, and how many in each craft? . . . .
(b) How many craft apprentices (if any) are directly employed? . . . .
(c) How many other operatives are permanently and directly employed? . . . .

12. Details of any trades which are normally sub-let . . . .

13. Give details of any trade/craft association of which company is a member . . . .

14. (a) How many permanent site supervisory staff are employed? (e.g. resident site foremen, etc.) . . . .
(b) How many visiting supervisory staff are employed? (State normal frequency of visits) . . . .
(c) Number and type of managerial/technical head office staff employed . . . .

15. (a) Name and value of the largest contract completed in the last two years

    . . . .
    . . . .

    (b) Name and value of the current largest ongoing contract

    . . . .
    . . . .

    (c) Brief details of the current smallest value contracts which are in hand

    . . . .
    . . . .

    (d) State minimum and maximum value of contracts in which interested

    Minimum £ . . . .
    Maximum £ . . . .

    (e) State preferred range of contract values

    £ . . . . to £ . . . .

16. (a) What is the nature of company's predominant workload? (e.g. general building, repairs and maintenance, speculative housing, etc.)

    . . . .
    . . . .

    (b) Of your company's annual turnover what proportion, in percentage terms, would you attribute to conservation work?

    Say . . . . %

17. (a) Give brief details of large mechanical plant owned by company (e.g. excavation equipment, lorries, etc.)

    . . . .
    . . . .

    (b) Give brief details of workshop equipment owned by company (e.g. joinery shop, fully equipped masonry yard, etc.)

    . . . .
    . . . .

18. Give brief details of specialist work which the company is able to carry out with its own permanently and directly employed labour (e.g. masonry, stone carving, flintwork, roof tiling and slating, thatching, hand finished traditional carpentry and joinery, sheet metal roofing, ornamental leadwork, wrought ironwork, decorative plasterwork, gilding and high class decorative work, etc.)

    . . . .
    . . . .
    . . . .
    . . . .

19. Brief details of any experience in refurbishment/conservation work associated with historic or listed buildings, old churches, and the like. (You may continue on a separate sheet if you wish)

    . . . .
    . . . .
    . . . .
    . . . .

20. Names and addresses of two of the company's clients who have placed orders for refurbishment/conservation work

    (1) . . . .
    . . . .
    . . . .
    Tel. no. . . . .
    (2) . . . .
    . . . .
    . . . .
    Tel. no. . . . .

21. Names and addresses of two firms of architects or chartered building surveyors, preferably practising in the conservation field, with whom your company has worked

    (1) . . . .
    . . . .
    . . . .
    Tel. no. . . . .
    (2) . . . .
    . . . .
    . . . .
    Tel. no. . . . .

22. Name and address of banker

    . . . .
    . . . .
    . . . .
    Tel. no. . . . .

23. Do you hereby grant authority for us to seek recommendations and/or references from those named in 20–2 above?

    YES/NO

24. List of sites that company would be willing to arrange for our representatives to inspect for standards of workmanship

    . . . .
    . . . .
    . . . .
    . . . .

Questionnaire for completion by specialists

Chapter 13 deals with the occasions when a structured questionnaire needs to be issued to potential tenderers. This appendix may be used as the basis for issue to specialists involved in conservation activities.

When dealing with specialists it is necessary to remember that some firms are extremely small. On occasion they comprise highly competent craftsmen who are not particularly good at completing questionnaires. It may therefore be necessary to offer guidance or even accept a less than perfectly completed form. This is particularly necessary if the specialist is otherwise found to be extremely competent in his craft.

CONFIDENTIAL   File ref. _____

QUESTIONNAIRE FOR SPECIALISTS WISHING TO BE CONSIDERED
FOR TENDERING ON CONSERVATION WORKS COMMISSIONED BY
(NAME OF ORGANIZATION)

---

1. Name of company   . . . .

2. Registered office   . . . .

                                . . . .

                                . . . .

                                Tel. no. . . . .

                                Fax no. . . . .

3. Local office   . . . .

                                . . . .

                                . . . .

                                Tel. no. . . . .

                                Fax no. . . . .

4. Nature of company and date
   established   ....

5. Status of company (e g. family
   business, partnership, sole   ....
   proprietor)   ....

6. (a) Type of work carried out
   (e.g. masonry, stone carving,
   flintwork, roof tiling and slating,
   thatching, hand finished
   traditional carpentry and
   joinery, sheet metal roofing,
   ornamental leadwork, wrought   ....
   ironwork, decorative
   plasterwork, gilding and high   ....
   class decorative work, etc.)   ....
   (b) Name of craft/trade
   association of which company   ....
   is a member   ....

7. Annual turnover (approx.)   £ ....

8. Name of parent or holding
   company (if applicable)   ....

9. Is company registered for VAT?
   (If yes, give registration no.)   ....

10. Give brief details of any third
    party insurance (e.g. name of   ....
    insurer and amount of cover)   ....

11. Geographical area in which
    work normally carried out
    (state radius from office)   ....

12. (a) How many craftsmen are
    permanently and directly
    employed?   ....
    (b) How many craft apprentices
    (if any) are directly employed?   ....

13. Brief details of site supervisory
    staff (please state if resident   ....
    on site or visiting)   ....

14. State minimum and maximum   Minimum £ ....
    value of contracts in which
    interested   Maximum £ ....

15. State preferred range of   £ .... to £ ....
    contract values

16. Brief details of any experience in refurbishment/conservation work associated with historic or listed buildings, old churches, and the like. (You may continue on a separate sheet if you wish)

....

....

....

....

....

17. Names and addresses of two of the company's clients/architects/chartered building surveyors who have placed orders for refurbishment/conservation work

(1) ....

....

....

Tel. no. ....

(2) ....

....

....

Tel. no. ....

18. Name and address of banker

....

....

....

Tel. no. ....

19. Do you hereby grant authority for us to seek recommendations and/or references from those named in 17. and 18. above?

YES/NO

20. List of sites that company would be willing to arrange for our representatives to inspect for standards of workmanship

....

....

....

....

....

Principal grant aid organizations and contacts

This appendix includes the principal organizations associated with the provision of grant aid for constructional activities. Several of the organizations listed operate on a countrywide basis and have a particular interest in the continued existence and upkeep of historic buildings, ancient monuments, townscapes and in conservation areas. Other organizations included will be more concerned with social and economic benefits and values; these may offer, therefore, grant aid for activities associated with traditional or old buildings which, in themselves, are not of great historic or architectural interest. In some instances statutory listing or scheduling will be a prerequisite to a project being considered for grant aid. Other circumstances will apply when statutory listing or scheduling is totally unnecessary.

Even if an organization is included in this appendix it is most likely that it will have insufficient funds available to meet all the demands made upon it. For this reason it is necessary to understand that any grant aid available is likely to be both variable and discretionary. At certain times funds available for grant aid become totally depleted simply because of the extent of requests for financial assistance from an ever-growing list of applicants. Because of the finite source of funding available, frequently made available through the public purse, there is an increasing tendency for the introduction of a greater degree of means testing to be applied. Clients should be made aware of the possibility of having to make disclosures about their financial affairs.

This appendix also includes a list of useful contacts and addresses. In this connection it should be noted that grant aid organizations and other contacts are likely to change their addresses from time to time. Similarly government departments are sometimes subject to a change in title although their functions may remain substantially unaltered.

The economic and political climate may also be responsible for changes in existing schemes, for schemes being abandoned, and for new schemes being introduced. For this reason suitably headed blank pages have been included in the appendix to enable the reader to insert his or her notes about such changes.

An example of change in legislation is that brought about by the Local Government and Housing Act 1989. This will progressively introduce changes to those local authority grants which are listed in this appendix. However, for some time it is likely that there will continue to be references to 'home improvement grants', 'home improvement: repair grants', and 'home improvement: intermediate grants'. Nevertheless there will be the need to become increasingly aware of a change to new terminology such as 'renovation grants', 'common parts grants', 'houses in multi-occupation grants', 'disabled persons grants', 'minor works grants' and 'group repair grants'. One of the principal changes, apart from terminology, will be an increased emphasis by local authorities on the need for applicants to contribute to the cost of approved repairs.

Another change is being brought about by the introduction of the Planning (Listed Buildings and Conservation Areas) Act 1990. This is a consolidated Act which will increasingly become a source of reference for those involved with listed buildings (or unlisted buildings which are of architectural or historic interest), for those associated with the preservation or enhancement of conservation areas, and for those with an involvement in town schemes. Because of the present common usage of the terms 'Section 3A', 'Section 10', 'Section 10B' and 'Section 24' grants, it has been decided to retain these well-known terms in the commentary columns of this appendix. However, with a greater familiarity of the new consolidated Act of 1990, the reader may become increasingly aware of references to passages or sections within the Planning (Listed Buildings and Conservation Areas) Act 1990 and which, in time, will supersede references to sections of earlier acts. For those who wish to make themselves familiar with the Planning Act 1990 the following chapters and sections may be of particular relevance.

Planning (Listed Buildings and Conservation Areas) Act 1990; Chapter 9

Part I

Chapter	Section	Content
V	47	Compulsory acquisition of listed buildings in need of repair
	48	Repairs notice as preliminary to acquisition
	49	Compensation on compulsory acquisition of listed building

Insofar as references to grants are concerned the reader's attention is directed particularly to Sections 57, 77 and 80 within the new Act. However, it must be emphasized that notwithstanding the introduction of a new Act the general principles which will guide applicants, their professional advisors, and those officials dealing with grant applications will remain substantially unaltered.

LOCAL AUTHORITY GRANTS

Grant type	Eligibility	Property type	Grant value	Comments
Historic Buildings	Private owners	Historic buildings; in need of repair and maintenance.	Unlikely to exceed 50% of cost of eligible repairs; generally less.	Applicable to listed buildings and others if of special interest; may include churches in use. Grant variable and discretionary, dependent on funds available.
Contact The relevant local authority.				
Home Improvement: Improvement Grant	Private owners and developers	Housing in need of substantial improvement	Unlikely to exceed 75% of cost of essential eligible improvements to make dilapidated housing suitable for occupation, but see comments for associated 'improvements'.	Applicable to older dilapidated housing unfit for occupation. Grant intended to aid essential improvements to make housing fit for occupation. Means tested. Tenants eligible if responsible for repairs. Grant normally available for essential eligible repairs up to pre-determined limits. Associated improvements may attract discretionary grant.
Contact The relevant local authority.				

LOCAL AUTHORITY GRANTS (cont'd)

Grant type	Eligibility	Property type	Grant value	Comments
Home Improvement: Repair Grant	Private owners and developers	Housing in need of substantial repair	Unlikely to exceed 75% of cost of essential eligible repairs to the main structure, but see comments for associated repairs.	Applicable to older dilapidated housing in need of repairs to the main structure. Routine maintenance to worn fixtures usually not eligible. Replacement of sanitary appliances and electrical wiring usually excluded. Means tested. Tenants eligible if responsible for repairs. Grant variable and discretionary. Associated repairs to other than foundations, walls, floors and roofs may qualify for additional discretionary grant.
Contact The relevant local authority.				

Grant type	Eligibility	Property type	Grant value	Comments
Home Improvement: Intermediate Grant	Private owners, developers and others	Housing lacking basic amenities	Unlikely to exceed 75% of cost of providing eligible basic amenities, but see comments for associated repairs.	Applicable to older housing lacking basic amenities such as WCs, sinks, baths, lavatory basins and hot and cold services. Means tested. Tenants eligible if responsible for repairs. Grant normally available up to certain limits. Associated repairs may attract discretionary grant.
Contact The relevant local authority				
Community Centres	A group approved by the local authority where the local inhabitants are the principal beneficiaries (e.g. a parish council)	Disused historic buildings or equivalent capable of conversion to community centres including facilities for entertainments and tourism.	Unlikely to exceed 50% of eligible conversion costs. Grant funded equally between the local authority and the sponsoring governmental source.	Applicable to disused historic buildings where there is a demand and need for conversion to centres of the type described. Buildings may require Listed Building Consent. The locally approved group is usually required to match the funding which may be available from local or governmental sources.
Contact The relevant local authority				

LOCAL AUTHORITY GRANTS (cont'd)

Grant type	Eligibility	Property type	Grant value	Comments
Town Scheme	Private owners or others within an existing town scheme or for the creation of a scheme. Town scheme grants are given through the agency of a local authority.	Any building located within an existing or proposed conservation area where there exists an agreement or proposal for joint funding between a governmental agency and the local authority towards comprehensive repairs for structural and external items within a designated area.	Generally not exceeding 40% of cost of eligible repairs shared equally between the governmental agency and local authority. On occasion may be the subject of higher 'special' grant.	A joint local authority and English Heritage (or equivalent) scheme; also referred to as a Section 10B grant. Applicable to any building provided the works comprise essential structural repairs to the main fabric of a building or to external features which contribute to the value of the group of buildings or townscape. It is expected that repairs will include traditional materials appropriate to the agreed 'town scheme' area. Eligible work may include repair or restoration of particular features such as railings, balustrades, chimney pots, sash windows and the like which contribute to the town

Grant type	Eligibility	Property type	Grant value	Comments
Town Scheme (cont'd) *Contact* The relevant local authority, English Heritage or equivalent governmental agency.				scheme. Grant variable and discretionary and related to eligible work only. Professional fees may qualify for grant up to prescribed limits in respect of eligible work only. *Note:* Also refer to English Heritage (or equivalent) direct grant to owners of buildings in conservation areas.

GOVERNMENTAL GRANTS: ENGLISH HERITAGE; CADW; HISTORIC SCOTLAND; NORTHERN IRELAND, DOE

Grant type	Eligibility	Property type	Grant value	Comments
Outstanding Buildings *Contact* The relevant governmental agency. Addresses and telephone numbers are included at the end of this appendix.	Private owners, companies, trusts, parochial church councils, local authorities and others	Outstanding buildings and places of worship in use (excluding scheduled ancient monuments and cathedrals). NB Those	Unlikely to exceed 40% of cost of eligible repairs for private owners and churches; this reduces to not exceeding 25% for	Also referred to as Section 3A grants. Applicable only to outstanding secular buildings and places of worship requiring

GOVERNMENTAL GRANTS: ENGLISH HERITAGE; CADW; HISTORIC SCOTLAND; NORTHERN IRELAND, DOE (cont'd)

Grant type	Eligibility	Property type	Grant value	Comments
Outstanding Buildings (cont'd)		buildings which qualify are generally listed Grade 1 or Grade 2*. Listing does not automatically mean a building will be admitted as outstanding.	local authorities. On occasion may be the subject of higher 'special' grant particularly if consideration is being given to taking the building into public care or guardianship.	major repairs to their historic fabric. Maintenance and routine repairs are excluded. Grant variable and discretionary and related to eligible work only. Professional fees may qualify for grant up to prescribed limits in respect of eligible work only.
Buildings at Risk	Private owners, amenity societies, preservation trusts, local authorities and others.	Outstanding buildings; also listed buildings in conservation areas. Properties are generally unoccupied and in neglected condition constituting an 'at risk' category.	Unlikely to exceed 25% (40% for truly outstanding buildings) of cost of urgent eligible repairs when in private or equivalent ownership. May be increased up to 50% for local authorities.	A special category applicable only to 'buildings at risk'. Grant to be used for effecting urgent and essential repairs to the basic structure to enable a building to survive. On occasion such buildings may be wilfully neglected or neglected through genuine inability to fund the cost of minimal but essential
Contact The relevant governmental agency. Addresses and telephone numbers are included at the end of this appendix.				

Grant type	Eligibility	Property type	Grant value	Comments
Buildings at Risk (cont'd)				repairs. Persistent and wilful neglect of a listed building may lead to service of an enforcement notice, the execution of minimum essential repairs, and the recovery of costs from the owner.
Scheduled Ancient Monuments	Private owners, companies, trusts, local authorities and others.	Scheduled ancient monuments.	Generally not exceeding 50% of cost of eligible repairs and consolidation. Reduces to 25% or less for local authorities.	Also referred to as Section 24 grants. Applicable only to scheduled ancient monuments for approved repairs and consolidation. Grant variable and discretionary and related to eligible work only. Archaeological scrutiny of proposals and work most likely. Professional fees may qualify for grant up to prescribed limits in respect of eligible work only.
Contact The relevant governmental agency. Addresses and telephone numbers are included at the end of this appendix.				

GOVERNMENTAL GRANTS: ENGLISH HERITAGE; CADW; HISTORIC SCOTLAND; NORTHERN IRELAND, DOE (cont'd)

Grant type	Eligibility	Property type	Grant value	Comments
Buildings in Conservation Areas	Private owners, amenity societies, preservation trusts, local authorities and others.	Any building located within a designated conservation area or equivalent where there is an approved scheme in operation or when a local authority has been invited to submit proposals for a programme of activities. The repairs must be of an approved type (see comments).	Generally not exceeding 25% of cost of eligible repairs but on occasion may be the subject of higher 'special' grant.	Also referred to as Section 10 grants. Applicable to any building provided the works comprise essential structural repairs to the main fabric of a building or to its historic or other special features. Not limited to listed buildings. It is expected that repairs will include traditional materials appropriate to the conservation area or to the village, street, terrace or square of which the building forms a part. Eligible work may include structural repairs and repairs or restoration of particular features such as railings, balustrades, chimney pots, sash windows and the like. Grant variable and discretionary and
Contact The relevant governmental agency. Addresses and telephone numbers are included at the end of this appendix.				

Grant type	Eligibility	Property type	Grant value	Comments
Buildings in Conservation Areas (cont'd)				related to eligible work only. Professional fees may qualify for grant up to prescribed limits in respect of eligible work only. NB Also refer to 'Town Scheme' grants administered by certain local authorities.
London Grants *Note:* In addition to 'London Grants' the London Region of English Heritage also administers grants for Scheduled Ancient Monuments, 'Town Schemes' and for 'Buildings in Conservation Areas'. See elsewhere for these other grants which are also applicable to the Greater London area. *Contact* The relevant governmental agency. Addresses and telephone numbers are included at the end of this appendix.	Private owners, companies, trusts, parochial church councils, local authorities and others.	Listed historic buildings. Must be located in the Greater London area.	Unlikely to exceed 50% of eligible cost of repairs.	Applicable only to listed buildings requiring repair work to enhance and/or protect the architectural or historic interest of a building. Grant may apply towards the repair or replacement of special features. Maintenance and routine repairs are excluded. Grant variable and discretionary and related to eligible work only. Professional fees may qualify for grant up to prescribed limits in respect of eligible work only.

GOVERNMENTAL GRANTS: RURAL DEVELOPMENT COMMISSION

Grant type	Eligibility	Property type	Grant value	Comments
Funded Partnership Scheme *Contact* The relevant governmental agency. Addresses and telephone numbers are included at the end of this appendix.	Charities, non-profit making trusts and local authorities.	Existing buildings capable of conversion to workshops or light industrial use.	Generally not exceeding 50% of cost of eligible work.	Applicable to any building within a rural development area. In planning terms is seen as an encouragement towards the creation of greater local social and economic benefits.
Grants for Village Halls *Contact* The relevant governmental agency. Addresses and telephone numbers are included at the end of this appendix.	Local voluntary committees.	Existing village community centres and village halls.	Generally not exceeding 25% of cost of eligible work up to prescribed limits.	Applicable to any existing village community centre or hall capable of alteration to the greater benefit of the local community. It is expected that local support can be clearly demonstrated.
Grants for Conversion of Redundant Buildings *Contact* The relevant governmental agency. Addresses and telephone numbers are included at the end of this appendix.	Private owners, local authorities and others.	Redundant rural buildings of any type.	Generally not exceeding 25% of cost of eligible repairs, alterations, and improvements up to prescribed limits.	Applicable to any redundant building within a rural development area which is capable of conversion to workshops, light industrial or similar uses. In planning

GOVERNMENTAL GRANTS: RURAL DEVELOPMENT COMMISSION (cont'd)

Grant type	Eligibility	Property type	Grant value	Comments
Grants for Conversion of Redundant Buildings (cont'd)				terms is seen as an encouragement towards the creation of greater local social and economic benefits.

GOVERNMENTAL GRANTS: MINISTRY OF AGRICULTURE AND FISHERIES (ENGLAND) AND WELSH, SCOTTISH AND NORTHERN IRELAND EQUIVALENTS

Grant type	Eligibility	Property type	Grant value	Comments
Reinstatement and Repair of Traditional Farm Buildings	Private owners and others; principally those with an active agricultural business.	Traditional farm buildings in active use.	Generally not exceeding 35% of cost of eligible repairs up to prescribed limits.	Applicable to any traditional farm building which is in active use. Intended to assist towards the rein-statement and retention of buildings in an active farming environment. Grant variable, discretionary and related to eligible work only.
Contact The relevant governmental department. Addresses and telephone numbers are included at the end of this appendix.				

GOVERNMENTAL GRANTS: THE SPORTS COUNCIL (ENGLAND) AND WELSH, SCOTTISH AND NORTHERN IRELAND EQUIVALENTS

Grant type	Eligibility	Property type	Grant value	Comments
Creating Sports Facilities *Contact* The relevant Regional Sports Council. Addresses and telephone numbers are included at the end of this appendix.	Private owners, local authorities and others.	Redundant buildings capable of being converted to provide additional sporting facilities.	Variable. Subject to assessment on a project basis.	Applicable to any redundant building which is capable of economic adaptation to provide enhanced or additional sporting facilities. Funds strictly limited. Grant variable, discretionary and only related to provision of enhanced or additional sporting facilities. Means tested.

OTHER SOURCES OF GRANT AID

Note: This tabulated page is provided to enable the reader to insert additional information about new and evolving schemes of grant aid.

Grant type	Eligibility	Property type	Grant value	Comments

USEFUL ADDRESSES

Grant type	Sponsor	Country	Address	Telephone
Historic Buildings	Local authorities	UK	County, city, borough or district councils (or equivalent) with jurisdiction over the locality involved. *Note:* Refer to particular local authority, public libraries, Thomson Local Directories, British Telecom Telephone Directories and British Telecom Yellow Pages and other sources for full addresses.	From same source as previous column.
Home Improvement: Improvement Grant				
Home Improvement: Repair Grant				
Home Improvement: Intermediate Grant				
Community Centres				
Town Schemes (in conjunction with governmental grants)				
Outstanding Buildings	English Heritage	England (excluding London)	*English Heritage, . . . Region, Fortress House, 23 Savile Row, London, W1X 1AB	071-973 3000
Buildings at Risk	English Heritage	England	*English Heritage, Buildings at Risk, Keysign House, 429 Oxford Street, London, W1R 2HD	071-973 3000
Scheduled Ancient Monuments	English Heritage	England (excluding London)	*English Heritage, . . . Region, Fortress House, 23 Savile Row, London, W1X 1AB	071-973 3000
Town Schemes	English Heritage	England (excluding London)	*English Heritage, . . . Region, Fortress House, 23 Savile Row, London, W1X 1AB	071-973 3000

Grant type	Sponsor	Country	Address	Telephone
Building in Conservation Areas	English Heritage	England (excluding London)	*English Heritage, ... Region, Fortress House, 23 Savile Row, London, W1X 1AB	071-973 3000
London Grants **Outstanding Buildings** **Scheduled Ancient Monuments** **Town Schemes** **Buildings in Conservation Areas**	English Heritage	England (London only)	*English Heritage, London Region, Chesham House, 30 Warwick Street, London, W1R 5RD	071-973 3000

* English Heritage has announced its intention to relocate to Nottingham in 1994/95 for most of its functions apart from those which relate to London Grants. All of the English Heritage addresses should therefore be treated with caution and it would be prudent to telephone their Headquarters building on 071-973 3000 to ensure that correspondence and telephone enquiries are directed to the correct location and number.

From 1 April 1991 grants outside London will be administered on a Regional basis. Applicants and their agents should, until relocation has been completed, address communications to the following contact points:

  North Region (for all counties north of Cheshire to Humberside);
  Midland Region (for all counties in the Midlands and East Anglia);
  South Region (for all counties in the South East and South West).

USEFUL ADDRESSES (cont'd)

Grant Type	Sponsor	Country	Address	Telephone
Outstanding Buildings **Buildings at Risk** **Scheduled Ancient Monuments** **Town Schemes**	Cadw and	Wales	Cadw, Welsh Historic Monuments, Brunel House, 2 Fitzalan Road, Cardiff, CF2 1UY	0222 465511
	Historic Scotland and	Scotland	Historic Scotland, 20 Brandon Street, Edinburgh, EH3 5RE	031 5568400
Buildings in **Conservation Areas**	Northern Ireland DOE	NI	Historic Monuments and Buildings Branch, Department of the Environment, Calvert House, 23 Castle Street, Belfast, BT1 1FY	0232 230560
Funded Partnership **Scheme**	Rural Development Commission and	England	Rural Development Commission, 141 Castle Street, Salisbury, SP1 3TI	0722 336255
Grants for Village **Halls**	Welsh Development Agency and	Wales	Welsh Development Agency, Pearl House, Greyfriars Road Cardiff, CF1 3XX	0222 222666
Grants for Conversion **of Redundant** **Buildings**	Scottish Development Agency and	Scotland	Scottish Development Agency, 120 Bothwell Street, Glasgow, G2 7JP	041-248 2700
	Rural Action Projects (NI)	NI	Rural Action Projects (NI), 10 Shipquay Street, Londonderry, BT48 6DN	0504 265241

Grant type	Sponsor	Country	Address	Telephone
Reinstatement/Repair of Traditional Farm Buildings	Ministry of Agriculture, Fisheries and Food	England	MAFF, Rural Structures and Grants Division, Nobel House, 17 Smith Square, London, SW1P 3HX	071-238 5644
	Welsh Office Agriculture Department	Wales	Welsh Office Agriculture Department, Cathay's Park, Cardiff, CF1 3NQ	0222 825111
	Department of Agriculture and Fisheries for Scotland and	Scotland	Department of Agriculture and Fisheries for Scotland, Pentland House, 47 Robbsloan, Edinburgh, EH14 1TW	031-556 8400
	Department of Agriculture for Northern Ireland	NI	Department of Agriculture for Northern Ireland, Dundonald House, Upper Newtownards Road, Belfast, BT4 3SB	0232 650111
Creating Sports Facilities	Sports Council and	England	Sports Council, 16 Upper Woburn Place, London, WC1H 0GP	071-388 1277
	Welsh Sports Council and	Wales	Welsh Sports Council, Plas-y-Brenin, Capel Curig, Betws-y-Coed, Gwynedd, LL24 0ET	0690 4214
	Scottish Sports Council and	Scotland	Scottish Sports Council, Caledonia House, South Gyle, Edinburgh, EH12 9DQ	031-317 7200
	Sports Council for Northern Ireland	NI	Sports Council for Northern Ireland, House of Sport, Upper Malone Road, Belfast, BT9 5LA	0232 381222

USEFUL ADDRESSES (cont'd)

Note: This tabulated page is provided to enable the reader to insert the addresses of additional or new sources of grant aid.

Grant Type	Sponsor	Country	Address	Telephone

Appendix G

Glossary of terms

Accepted Risks Those risks accepted by a client and from which a contractor is absolved.

Advances on Account *See* Payments on account.

Alterations, additions and omissions *See* Variations (VOs).

Antiquities *See* Archaeological finds.

Arbitration A means of resolving disputes without recourse to the Courts.

Archaeologist A person skilled in the recognition and identification of ancient or historic remains. *See also* Inspector.

Archaeological finds Antiquities or historic remains of a previously unknown nature which are discovered on site.

Architect A professional skilled in the architectural design disciplines. Must be registered to use the title 'architect'.

Artist An individual who undertakes or performs a work of art or carries out an artistic activity as opposed to a normal craft operation. Those who undertake work such as carving or sculpture may variously claim to be either artists or craftsmen. *See also* Conservators.

Authority *See* Client.

Bills of quantities; generally A contractual pricing document used by tenderers to calculate their tender offers. Also used for valuations and final accounts.

Bills of quantities; approximate A bill of quantities where the descriptions are generally applicable to the work to be performed but where the quantities or extent of the work is substantially subject to assessment.

Bills of quantities; firm A bill of quantities prepared for a substantially pre-planned project.

Bills of quantities; provisional A bill of quantities where both the descriptions of work to be performed and the quantities or extent of the work are principally conjectural.

Building surveyor A professional whose skills are particularly relevant to the preparation of drawings and specifications for work of alteration and repair. Also skilled at inspections and the survey of buildings.

Certificate; for payment An SO's written statement informing the client that an interim or final payment in a particular sum is due to the contractor.

Certificate; for practical completion An SO's written statement confirming that the works are effectively complete and in a condition ready for handover to the client.

Certificate; of making good defects An SO's written statement to the effect that all defects which have occurred during the maintenance period and notified to the contractor have been made good to the SO's satisfaction.

Certificates; others The conditions of contract may refer to the SO's power or duty to issue certificates in respect of other matters. A certificate in respect of an authorized extension of time is such an example.

Civil engineer A professional skilled in the theory and practice of engineering design particularly related to earthworks and heavy or complex engineering structures.

Claims; generally A submission by the contractor for extra monies which are initially repudiated or in dispute.

Claims; contractual A claim submitted by a contractor which is related to a clause in the conditions of contract.

Claims; extra contractual A claim submitted by a contractor which has no foundation under the terms of the conditions of contract but where there may be an entitlement at Common Law.

Claims; *ex gratia* A claim submitted by a contractor which has no validity under the terms of the contract or at Common Law but where the claimant seeks to show that he has suffered loss and claims recovery by placing himself at the mercy of the client.

Clerk of works A person generally trained as a craftsman, with wide experience, and normally resident on site, who acts on behalf of the client in inspecting, approving or rejecting materials and workmanship. Usually acts under the directions of the SO. May carry out other delegated functions.

Client The person or organization initiating a project and who is responsible for paying the contractor. One of the two customary signatories to a contract. Also referred to as 'the authority' or 'the employer'.

Conditions of contract A set of conditions or clauses which define the responsibilities, liabilities and rights of both client and contractor insofar as a contract is concerned. Others such as the SO, quantity surveyor and clerk of works may be referred to in the conditions. A series of different standard conditions are available and the most appropriate should be selected for a proposed contract.

Conservators   Those with recognized skills in dealing with works of art such as furniture, tapestries, paintings and other interior furnishings. Usually specialize in particular objects. *See also* Artist.

Consolidation   The term given to the in-situ repair of existing ancient monuments or historic buildings so that their original state is not impaired. It does not extend to include alterations, extensions or improvements.

Contingencies   A sum which is earmarked or set aside to meet possible expenditure for unknown factors which may be encountered on a contract once work is proceeding on site. Also used to meet the cost of possible changes required by a client and to help defray the cost of any mistakes or omissions in contract documentation where a contractor has an entitlement to extra payment.

Contract   An agreement between the parties for work to be performed in return for an agreed sum or for a sum which is capable of calculation under the terms of the contract. May be verbal but usually in writing.

Contractor   An individual, firm or organization capable of performing works activities and of entering into contracts for their execution. Generally applied to those capable of performing a wide range of skilled activities and/or able to co-ordinate, manage and supervise a complete project.

Cost plus contracts   *See* Prime cost contracts.

Daily returns   Those returns required of a contractor which detail all significant movements of labour, materials and plant to and from the site. May or may not be in conditions of contract.

Damages   *See* Liquidated damages.

Date for completion   An agreed date or period of time entered in a contract. May be varied by an authorized extension of time (qv) or by mutual agreement.

Daywork   Payment for work performed on a cost-plus basis. A contractor is reimbursed for all labour, materials and plant employed, together with allowances for overheads and profit. Difficult to monitor.

Daywork term contract   A contract for a given period of time where payment is made on the basis of daywork.

Defects liability period   A period stated in a contract during which time a contractor has to rectify, at his own expense, any defects in materials or workmanship which are notified to him and which are not in accordance with the contract requirements. The defects liability period commences at the date of practical completion and runs for a pre-determined period (frequently 6 months).

Determination (of a contract) An invoked ending of a contract before its completion.

Directly employed labour (DEL) Craftsmen and other employees paid for direct, usually on a full-time basis, by the client, authority or employer.

Designer A convenient term used throughout this book to describe the person or organization responsible for the design of a project. It is equally applicable to architects, building surveyors, civil engineers, structural engineers or others with the responsibility for the design and/or specification of the works.

Design team The term used to embrace all those professionals and others jointly or severally engaged on a construction project on behalf of a client.

Direct contractor An individual or firm appointed direct by the client to perform activities contemporaneously with the contractor. They are not in a contractual relationship with the contractor.

Disruption and prolongation Circumstances which may lead to an entitlement or claim for extra monies by a contractor.

Drawings Drawing information showing the work to be performed and supplementary information such as site location, access routes and similar matters. Should always be provided but not all drawings have the status of a contract document particularly if the work can be fully described in other ways.

Electrical engineer A term used to denote a professional skilled in the design and supervision of electrical works.

Eligible work A term used in grant aid. That part of the works which is eligible for financial assistance.

Employer *See* Client.

Extension of time An extension to the contract period as authorized and certified by the SO.

Final account A document, usually in great detail, setting out the final sum payable to the contractor by the client after all authorized and agreed financial adjustments have been made to the original contract sum. Prior to agreement, the document is referred to as the draft final account.

Final certificate An SO's certificate issued to the client, frequently copied to the contractor, stating the final sum due to the contractor in full and final settlement of a contract.

Firm price tender *See* Tender; firm price.

Fluctuating tender *See* Tender; fluctuating price.

General contractor *See* Contractor.

Governmental Appertaining to government. A commission or similar authority or agency in the public sector which has close ties with a Government Department.

Grant aid Discretionary financial assistance to a building owner. Most assistance is publicly funded. Grant aid may take the form of lump sum contributions or loans towards part or the total cost of a project. Payments are limited to 'eligible' work. Grant aid is conditional.

Historian A person knowledgeable in history. In this book it denotes a particular knowledge of the historic aspects of buildings which is frequently relevant to conservation work. Conservation historians often work in close liaison with archaeologists.

Interim certificate *See* Certificates; for payment.

Interim payment *See* Payment on account.

Interim valuation *See* Valuation.

Inspector A term used to denote an inspector of ancient monuments. Generally an archaeologist by training (see Archaeologist). Usually possesses the experience to advise on appropriate means of consolidation in a historic context.

Instructions See under SO's Instructions.

Jobbing Work which, by its nature, is small in quantity and value.

Landscape architect A professional skilled in landscape design including associated planting. Some landscape architects have a knowledge of historic gardens.

Leave as found The term used in conservation which relates to the need to leave archaeological or historic artefacts undisturbed whenever possible so as not to destroy their authenticity and value.

Liquidated damages A pre-determined sum inserted in a contract which represents the genuine financial loss a client would suffer and which would be recoverable from the contractor in the event of late completion. Must not constitute a penalty.

Lump sum contract A contract for an agreed amount of work in return for a stipulated lump sum of money. See also under Tender – firm price and fluctuating price.

Main contractor   *See* Contractor.

Maintenance period   *See* Defects liability period.

Management fee contract   A contract where a contractor agrees to manage and procure all the services required in performing a project for a client in return for an agreed fee.

Measured term contract (MTC)   A contract let for an agreed period of time and with reimbursement related to measurement and payment for the work performed on the basis of a pre-determined schedule of rates. Should include updating provisions.

Mechanical engineer   A term used to denote a professional skilled in the design and supervison of heating, ventilating, hot water, cold water and similar services.

Non-completion (of a contract)   A breach of contract. There may be an entitlement to damages for breach of contract in the event that a contract does not include liquidated damages for late completion.

Omissions, alterations and additions   See under SO's instructions and variations.

Partial possession   A right which is written into some contracts for a client to take previously undeclared possession of any part of the works before completion of the whole. Not to be confused with stipulated phased completion which may be written into a contract at tender stage.

Parties to a contract   The client and contractor who have jointly agreed to enter into a contract.

Payment; on account   Money paid to a contractor during the progress of the works. Further payment usually falls due at practical completion and, following the making good of any defects, at the expiry of the defects liability period.

Payment; on completion   A payment which falls due when the works have been completed, any defects made good, and the final account agreed.

Phased completion   Any section of the works which is required by the contract to be executed and handed over to the client in advance of completion of the whole. Also referred to as sectional completion.

Plant   The term used to describe the equipment provided by a contractor to assist in performing the works. Plant may be described as 'mechanical' i.e. capable of movement or having a moving or 'live' part or described as 'non-mechanical' when it is in the form of hand tools, temporary buildings, scaffolding and other inanimate apparatus or objects.

Practical completion A contract stage where the works have progressed to the point when a client may reasonably take beneficial occupation. Usually denoted by the issue of an SO's Certificate of Practical Completion.

Preliminaries Those items of likely or possible cost to a contractor which are not a readily discernible part of the permanent work to be performed. More particularly it covers the general obligations and responsibilities of a contractor under a contract.

Prime cost contract A cost-plus contract where a contractor is reimbursed his actual costs plus either a fixed fee or a percentage addition. There is no initial contract sum.

Prime cost sum (PC sum) An amount included in Bill of Quantities or specifications for work to be performed or for materials to be supplied on the specific nomination of the SO.

Prolongation and disruption See under disruption and prolongation.

Provisional quantities Work included in a Bill of Quantities by way of assessment insofar as the quantities or extent of the work to be performed is concerned. Subject to financial adjustment in the final account when the actual quantities are known.

Provisional sum A sum included in a Bill of Quantities or specification for speculative activities which may be required or for work of an unknown nature/value. Subject to omission or financial adjustment in the final account when the nature and agreed value is known.

Quantities *See* Bills of quantities.

Quantity surveyor A professional whose skills are particularly directed to the measurement and valuation of constructional activities at all stages and who can best advise on the most appropriate means of contracting and tendering. Also referred to as a building cost consultant or building economist.

Reserve A sum earned by a contractor but which is kept back for payment until a later date in accordance with the conditions of contract. Usually one half of the reserve is released upon the issue of a Certificate of Practical Completion and the remaining reserve is released when the final certificate is issued by the SO.

Resident engineer A skilled technician or professional who is employed on the client's behalf on site to supervise the engineering activities of a contractor. Usually acts under the direction of and liaises with the SO.

Retention   *See* Reserve.

Returns; daily   *See* Daily returns.

Risks; accepted   *See* Accepted risks.

Schedule of rates   A priced list of works activities. Usually comprehensive and often voluminous.

Schedule of works/repairs   A list of activities to be performed. Often in tabulated format. Particularly useful for repetitive items.

Sectional completion   *See* Phased completion.

Site   The location where the works are to take place. Will include any area allocated for the temporary occupation of the contractor.

SO   See Superintending Officer.

SO's instructions   Any instruction which the SO is empowered or required to give under the terms of the conditions of contract.

Specialist   An individual or firm capable of carrying out specialist activities, frequently of a single craft nature, which are not normally performed by a contractor. May or may not be appointed as a nominated sub-contractor or listed as a named sub-contractor. Specialists will come under the general control of a contractor if they are nominated or named but not if appointed direct by the client as a direct contractor.

Specification   A description of materials to be provided and workmanship to be performed in carrying out a works project. May incorporate preliminaries (qv). Should always be provided but not always stipulated as a contract document.

Structural engineer   A professional skilled in the theory and practice of engineering design particularly related to foundations, masonry walling, concrete structures, steel and timber framing.

Sub-contractor; domestic   A firm selected and employed direct by a contractor to perform work on his behalf. Contractually a domestic sub-contractor has no special status and should be regarded in all respects as part of a contractor's own organization. Customary to obtain the SO's approval before employing a domestic sub-contractor on site.

Sub-contractor; named   One of a number of firms named in a specification or bill of quantities as being a firm a contractor is permitted or required to employ as a domestic sub-contractor.

Sub-contractor; nominated   A firm capable of providing particular materials or performing specialist work on the selection and nomination of the SO. A contractor is required to enter into a sub-contract agreement with the nominated firm and thereafter be responsible for the co-ordination of their activities. Nominations usually arise in respect of matters covered by PC sums.

Superintending officer (SO) A convenient and frequently used term to denote the person acting on the client's behalf in supervising and controlling a building or civil engineering project. Is applicable to the person who performs the function irrespective of their discipline or background. Some conditions of contract use the term 'architect' or 'engineer' when acting in the capacity described.

Supplementary conditions of contract Supplements and amendments to or ommisions from standard conditions of contract. Are sometimes necessary to meet particular client requirements. Need great care in drafting.

Tender; generally A formal quotation to perform work. Usually required to be submitted on a prescribed form.

Tender; firm price A lump sum firm price offer where the contractor is required to accept the risk of fluctuations in the cost of labour and materials.

Tender; fluctuating price A tender where the contractor is able to recover certain fluctuations in the cost of labour and materials. Similarly the client may be able to recover decreases which occur. Also referred to as a variation of price contract.

Value added tax (VAT) A Government imposed tax which may or may not apply to constructional activities depending on the legislation in force at the time of the contract. Is customary to exclude VAT from tender offers since the application and level of VAT is outside the control of the contracting parties. Thereafter VAT may become payable to the contractor by the client depending on the rates applicable at the time of performing the works.

Valuation The assessment of monies properly due to a contractor under the terms of the conditions of contract. A valuation leads to the issue of an appropriate Certificate for Payment (qv) and thence to payments on account and payment on completion (qv).

Variations (VOs) SO's instructions which vary the work of a contractor or his sub-contractors. Most conditions of contract empower the SO to issue instructions in respect of variations (commonly referred to as variation orders or VOs).

Variation of price tender *See* Tender; fluctuating price.

Works The works to be performed under a contract which are shown on the drawings and described in the bills of quantities and/or specification, including any additional extra or modified work required or any work omitted on the instructions of the SO.

Index